GOD'S WORD: BULLETPROOF

Prophetic Fulfillment, Archaeological Evidence, Science, and Common Sense Reasoning Prove the Bible

MICHAEL H. IMHOF
U.S. Navy SEAL Commander (Ret.)

ASPECT Books
www.ASPECTBooks.com

World rights reserved. This book or any portion thereof may not be copied or reproduced in any form or manner whatever, except as provided by law, without the written permission of the publisher, except by a reviewer who may quote brief passages in a review.

The author assumes full responsibility for the accuracy of all facts and quotations as cited in this book. The opinions expressed in this book are the author's personal views and interpretations, and do not necessarily reflect those of the publisher.

This book is provided with the understanding that the publisher is not engaged in giving spiritual, legal, medical, or other professional advice. If authoritative advice is needed, the reader should seek the counsel of a competent professional.

Copyright © 2021 Michael H. Imhof
Copyright © 2021 ASPECT Books
ISBN-13: 978-1-4796-1347-2 (Paperback)
ISBN-13: 978-1-4796-1348-9 (ePub)
Library of Congress Control Number: 2020920125

All Bible texts are taken from the King James Version (KJV) of the Bible unless otherwise stated. Public domain.

Scripture quotations marked (NKJV) are taken from the New King James Version. Copyright © 1982 by Thomas Nelson. Used by permission. All rights reserved.

The website references in this book have been shortened using a URL shortener and redirect service called 1ref.us, which ASPECT Books manages. If you find that a reference no longer works, please contact us and let us know which one is not working so that we can correct it. Any personal website addresses that the author included are managed by the author. ASPECT Books is not responsible for the accuracy or permanency of any links.

Published by

www.ASPECTBooks.com

"This riveting account of evidence and discovery brings the Bible to life. Readers will be thirsty for more as the author blends his personal experience of exploring the Middle East with archeological and scriptural research. Its clearly prepared pages will draw your mind to Christ and inspire you to dig deeper."

—*Timothy Hullquist/Consultant*

"*Get Ready!* Commander Michael Imhof will take you along with him reliving his many exciting trips throughout the Middle East, showing you all these places Almighty God and Jesus (Elohim) spoke of in the Holy Bible. Commander Imhof shows us how history and science confirm the Truth, quoting the Word of God. *Could not put this book down!*"

—*John A. Sterba, M.D., Ph.D., FACEP/Missionary, Saved by Grace Ministry, Inc./Commander, Medical Corps, USNR (Hon. Dis.)*

"I was '**touched emotionally and intellectually**' as I imagined walking along with Commander Michael Imhof as I read his words in this book. Through his dissertation, I saw the Lord at work setting up markers that would stand throughout history. There were times when I had to stop and ponder what I had just read in order to digest the words, and then enthusiastically reread them.

'**This is a book to be handed out to people of all levels of faith and walks of life.**'

Michael's other writings have been used throughout the world, and I pray for the Lord's doors to be open for this book in order to draw many to God's goodness and authenticity."

—*Patricia Plummer, President/Founder of Heart of Prayer Ministries, Inc., marketplace nonprofit ministry to business, government, and school leaders*

"Michael Imhof is a tremendous man of God. He is extremely knowledgeable of God's Word as well as being a great writer. His new book, *"God's Word: Bulletproof,"* was **'exceptionally enjoyable'**. I would be proud to have this book among my library of references. Reading this brought back fond memories of my trip to the Holy Land a few years ago. I'm sure I will refer to places and events in this book many times."

—*Loyce Webb/Sr. Pastor*

"Commander Michael Imhof's strong Christian values are evident in this easy-to-read, scripture-based book. Commander Imhof's personal travels backdrop key Bible passages; like his views of Mt. Sinai and the location of Noah's Ark as well as his confirmation of the Genesis account of Sodom and Gomorrah through archeological offerings. **'Do not miss the opportunity to reinforce your own Christian values'** through the well-documented contents of this book."

—*Chet Truskowski/Executive (ret.)/Chairman of Board (former)/ Bishop's Advisory Development Board Diocese Member*

"Commander Michael Imhof (ret.) writes in a conversational style which encourages the reader to accompany him as he reminisces of his past journeys into the biblical region of the Middle East. In doing so, he is reminded of significant biblical prophecies and events that have emphasized on the gospel—the Lord Jesus Christ himself. This **'book continues to underscore the veracity of God's Word as well as His faithfulness in keeping His Word.'** Imhof further supports his understanding of the biblical prophecies with relevant historical accounts and written archaeological evidences. From a military analogy and scientific perspective, God's Word is indeed bulletproof to any intent to 'steal, kill, and destroy' the God-designed truths."

—*Rev. Dr. Rachel Rajagopal/Founder, Faith Ablaze International Ministries/Ambassador, Acacia Mission/ Langham Author (Unashamed Servant-Leadership)*

"People today struggle more and more with the adage 'can you believe what you're being told, taught or sold?' Commander Imhof gives a unique approach toward securing the perimeter of confidence you can have in the Bible/gospel message. The reader gets to experience, through the author's eyes, his own personal experiences when traveling in the Middle East. You are presented with historical, archeological, scientific, and biblical proofs that bring comfort as you realize all that God has done in order to substantiate His Word, His Son, and His Message. I personally found *God's Word: Bulletproof* to be on target, bringing enlightening information, and resulting in increased comfort, and assurance towards my own faith.

If you're searching, and/or questioning the validity of the Bible, or the gospel message, **this book is for you**; if you feel inadequate or ill equipped to give a reasonable defense for your faith, **this book is for you**! If you're desiring more comforting assurance that what you're believing in is solid and true, **this book is for you**."

—*Mark Berney/Sr. Pastor*

"As a Police Officer for over 40 years and a retired Chief of Police, I value the direct and straightforward approach Commander Michael Imhof uses in his writing style. I have heard the Commander speak on various subjects, and while reading this book, I can hear his voice in every sentence he wrote. I perceived, while reading the Bible Scriptures cited in support of his research, that the '**passages were resonating with direct knowledge from God.**' The cited passages and his research would prove beyond any reasonable doubt in a court of law that these events took place, and that there was divine intervention influencing the course of history.

I '**highly recommend**' this book as a primer to anyone new to true Christianity. I also '**highly recommend**' this book as a reference document for anyone who is an avid reader of the Bible."

—*Nick Ficarello/Chief of Police (ret.)*

"Commander Imhof has done an '**excellent job**' of providing condensed points of proof in demonstrating that the Bible cannot be explained in any other way except via supernatural origin. His personal touch, relative to his extensive travels in the land of the Book, only adds to the intrigue and validity of the content of what he writes. The reader will be amazed by how rational it is to trust this ancient text."

—*Carl Wagner/Sr. Pastor*

"Mike has compiled an excellent resource of clear, concise material that conveys to the reader the veracity of the Bible. "**Highly recommended**," particularly for those engaged in ministry, and others as well."

—*Peter Outar/Sr. Pastor*

"Many years in communication roles as a trial lawyer, college professor and commentator, conditioned me when examining a new book or essay to think first and foremost about *credibility*. For a thinking person and a sincere truth-seeker a work of dubious credibility has little merit even though it may have "dramatic appeal" or some other meretricious attribute that would lead people to read it. But some of us have no interest in any work that cannot withstand the scrutiny aimed at determining the credibility of the author and his work.

Commander Imhof's book, ***God's Word: Bulletproof***, passes the credibility test.

Indeed, the credibility and the background of the author is perhaps the book's greatest asset. Very few human beings can lay claim to the achievements and experiences of Commander Imhof. He sees our world from a rare, if not unique, perspective, and one certainly not generally perceived as "religious." But that enhances the credibility factor.

That perspective, the subject of this book, and Commander Imhof's purposes in writing it, place it perhaps in a genre of one. I dare say there is no other book even similar to this.

The author recognized that throughout the 19th, 20th, and early 21st Centuries, archaeology and history have been, piece by piece with no plan or intent, disassembling the edifice of secular unbelief. New revelations in each discipline have been debunking the views and arguments of the secular minded, the unbelieving, the skeptical. No longer are Sodom and Gomorrah myths contrived to teach a moral lesson; they are scenes east of the Dead Sea littered with bones, ash and the evidences of fiery destruction. It is becoming, as Commander Imhof shows, more and more difficult to be simultaneously "scientific" and unbelieving. Indeed, it seems a new pseudo religion has been gradually devised to sustain many in their determined and purposeless opposition to faith.

But for those who are searching for Truth, not corroboration of prejudices or ideological fallacies, Commander Imhof offers up facts and analysis buttressed with logic, tying it all very conveniently together with pertinent Scripture. That aggregation of Biblical authority alone is a service to the reader.

God's Word: Bulletproof is a warrior's way—and of all people, warriors must deal in reality—of demonstrating something of immense value to the author: his own faith. It surely will affirm the faith of those who already believe, and most importantly, create in the minds of skeptics reasons not for doubt but for belief. In either case, it will have served a great purpose."

—*Ivy Scarborough/Lawyer/former University Professor of International Studies and History, and author*
(Into the Night—The Crisis of Western Civilization)

"A few weeks ago a member of my church shared with me a recent experience he had while doing ministry on the campus of one of our major universities. A young man he had told about the amazing love of God paused and asked him with sincerity, 'How do you know it's all true? How do you truly know?' This is a question burning in the hearts of many, if not most, people in the world today. They ask in their heart and mind, 'What is true?' 'Where can I find true, authentic answers?' Though there is very little evidence of the truth of God, His Son, and His Word more powerful than the testimony of a truly changed life, I wish my friend would have had a copy of this book to share with this young man seeking to know the truth. It is short, concise, straightforward, and compelling. The Bible is truth, and if you're intellectually honest with yourself, the evidence is there and irrefutable.

One reason I very much enjoyed Michael Imhof's book, **God's Word: Bulletproof** is the fresh, personal approach he takes in tackling questions about the veracity of the Bible. There are many books defending the accuracy of Scripture, but Commander Imhof does a great job in presenting factual evidence in a crisp, clear, and understandable manner, reflecting his years as a military commander and leader. His understanding of Scripture, combined with his personal observations while traveling extensively throughout the land of the Bible, is interwoven with archeological discoveries, scientific fact, and other historical evidence to create **an easy-to-read, easy-to-understand, and easy-to-believe defense of the Bible. In a world filled with people questioning the concept of absolute truth, who deep down are looking for answers and longing for something in this life to be real, lasting, and eternal, this book will absolutely help them by pointing them towards God and the truth of His Word.**"

—*Scott Tishler/Sr. Pastor*

Dedicated to all Christian missionaries worldwide. May their sacrifices be honored, and may their efforts show forth fruit throughout eternity as they shared the gospel and love of Jesus Christ to many.

"All scripture is given by inspiration of God,
and is profitable for doctrine, for reproof, for correction,
for instruction in righteousness."

2 Timothy 3:16

"But the word of the Lord endureth for ever. And this is
the word which by the gospel is preached unto you."

1 Peter 1:25

"Heaven and earth shall pass away,
but my words shall not pass away."

Matthew 24:35

"For the invisible things of him from the creation of the
world are clearly seen, being understood by the things
that are made, even his eternal power and Godhead;
so that they are without excuse."

Romans 1:20

Table of Contents

Foreword . . . . *xiii*

Acknowledgments . . . . *xv*

Introduction . . . . *xvi*

Section One—Prophetic Fulfillment

Chapter 1: Garden Tomb and Resurrection 20

Chapter 2: Jesus and Golgotha 24

Chapter 3: Tyre, Lebanon 29

Chapter 4: Memphis, Egypt 33

Chapter 5: Ammon 36

Chapter 6: Edom 38

Chapter 7: Babylon 43

Chapter 8: Nineveh 47

Chapter 9: Samaria 50

Chapter 10: Jericho 53

Chapter 11: Israel 56

Chapter 12: Chorazin, Capernaum, Bethsaida, Tiberius 61

Chapter 13: Cyrus 64

Chapter 14: King Zedekiah 67

Chapter 15: Josiah 70

Section Two—Archeological Evidence

Chapter 16: Mount Sinai 74
Chapter 17: Noah's Ark 81
Chapter 18: Damascus 85
Chapter 19: Sodom and Gomorrah 87
Chapter 20: Hazor, Megiddo, Shiloh 90
Chapter 21: Dead Sea Scrolls 94

Section Three—Science and Common Sense Reasoning

Chapter 22: Evolution versus Creationism 98
Chapter 23: Grand Canyon and Biblical Flood . . . 102
Chapter 24: Science Supports Noah's Flood 104
Chapter 25: Noah's Flood and the Great Ice Age . . . 106
Chapter 26: God Has Revealed Himself to Creation . . . 109
Chapter 27: Humans Created in the Image of God . . . 111
Chapter 28: Breath of Life 114
Chapter 29: The Bible 116

Section Four—Miscellaneous Commentaries

Chapter 30: Prophecy and Calculations 120
Chapter 31: Discovery of Oil in Israel? 124
Chapter 32: The Shroud of Turin 128

Conclusion 132
About the Author 134
Additional Books by Author 136
Contact Information 139

Foreword

As we proceed in life, sometimes we ponder memories from times past. All have memories. As for me, I was recently pondering how God allowed me to live and travel throughout the Middle East in some of my earlier years of life while in the military and as a civilian in support of paramilitary operations.

During these experiences, I would be exposed to some amazing biblical and associated locations. As I visited numerous interesting and varied sites in the performance of my duties, and during my free time, I came to realize something exceptionally unique about the Bible. There is no holy book in the world that deals accurately with prophecy except the Bible. If you find one, please let me know because I haven't found any. The Bible stands alone because the Bible is the inspired Word of God.

There's something about truth. Truth is absolute, and it always proves its course, and such it is with history and archeological evidence. History and archeological evidence back up the Bible again and again. To see what God said in His Word would happen, and then to see His Word confirmed with what transpired is supernaturally amazing.

For those people who say, prove to me that the Bible is true, I'm apt to say prove to me that it's not. As one looks at history, archeological evidence, science, and common sense reasoning, and then studies the Bible, one can only conclude that the Bible is, in fact, the inspired Word of God.

If we were in a court of law, and this case was brought before the court, the judge would realize that the evidence would overwhelmingly support the Bible as the inspired Word of God. God backs up His Word because God always honors His Word. History, archeological evidence, science, and common sense reasoning steadfastly sing in unison to this truth.

Michael H. Imhof
Commander, U.S. Navy (ret.)

Acknowledgments

Special thanks to Patricia Plummer and Colleen Biffert for administrative review and support.

Introduction

Get ready for your flight to the Middle East. Flight 1128 is now boarding for Tel Aviv, with a brief stop in Paris en route. At the same time, be aware that this flight is going to take you back into the history of this region. Many things will be examined through the eyes of history, archeological evidence, science, and common sense reasoning.

As a young Christian, I was excited to get my first overseas assignment as a Navy Lieutenant to the United Nations Truce Supervision Organization (UNTSO). During this assignment as a military observer, I would be assigned for duty in Egypt, Jordan, Israel, and work in Southern Lebanon as well. Further, during my free time, I would travel extensively throughout this region.

Later, in time, I would be assigned to the Multinational Force Organization (MFO) as a civilian observer. I would live at North Camp in the Sinai and conduct aerial and land operations in the performance of my duties. As such, I traveled extensively throughout the Sinai, eastern Egypt, and southern Israel.

What remarkable experiences I had in these assignments. Geographically, the Bible became alive to me. Further, in these ventures, I saw how history and archeological evidence consistently backed up the Bible time and time again. Not that God needed an apologetic to support His Word, but these personal experiences showed me that, although man records history, God writes it.

Numerous times I would become elated on where I was visiting while examining the history and archeological data of these varied locations.

The handprint of God was continuously in evidence over these remnants of time. That said, these varied events spoke volumes, when coupled with history and archeological evidence, of the veracity of God's Word.

I came to realize that the Bible was not a "pie in the sky" book, but that it was alive and breathed the air of truth. I'm so thankful that God gave me these experiences.

Now, travel with me back in time as I share these experiences with you. May you experience the same excitement, and receive the revelation of God's Word, perhaps in ways you haven't experienced before.

Section One—

Prophetic Fulfillment

The Garden Tomb

Chapter 1

Garden Tomb and Resurrection

∙∙∙

Many have visited the Garden Tomb. Excursions to Israel are done on an ongoing basis from the United States and many parts of the world. Of course, the Garden Tomb is typically on everyone's list to visit, and rightly so. As one visits, it's easy to make some conclusions as one goes back in time.

First, we know from scripture that the disciples were fearful for their lives. They fled for their lives when Jesus was taken in the Garden of Gethsemane; although, Peter followed along at a distance.

Second, these were fishermen, or comparable blue-collar workers, not trained in the art of war. We know from scripture that a large stone, millstone, or sealer, was placed at the opening of the tomb with a Roman guard. These fearful disciples, if they were to take the body, would have had to penetrate the guard, move the huge rock, and do so in a clandestine manner so as not to be noticed by the Roman guard. Not likely.

Third, the Roman Army was the premier force in the world at this time. These were trained soldiers given a mission. Guard the tomb. They were used to carrying out orders. It's not likely that the disciples could have penetrated the Roman guard without not being noticed if they were to try to take the body.

Fourth, let's consider Peter. Peter denied Jesus three times as he carefully followed the unfolding of events. He was afraid to even be associated with Jesus when others accused him of being with Jesus. This is an interesting observation to support the resurrection of Jesus Christ. I say this because, after the resurrection, when Peter sees Jesus face to face, he becomes bold after being empowered by the Holy Spirit. Peter would lead many to Christ, and according to tradition, eventually, be crucified upside down in Rome for his faith. Now, if Jesus had stayed in the tomb, Peter, already having denied Jesus, would have gone back to his fishing business in the Galilee region. This is a pretty easy conclusion.

Fifth, consider Saul of Tarsus, who later became known as Paul. Paul, an exceptionally well-educated Pharisee in the traditions of the law, aggressively persecuted Christians. He even held garments for those who stoned Stephen when Stephen was martyred. Paul was on his way to Damascus to persecute more Christians when he had his "Damascus Road" experience. As he was blinded by this bright light for a season of time, he realized that Jesus was talking to him and quickly changed his attitude about Christianity. Paul, a devout oppressor of Christians, would go on to become an outstanding man of God, and become the primary writer of the New Testament. Why the change, Paul? It's because Paul had an encounter with the resurrected Christ. Paul, according to tradition, would later in future years suffer a martyr's death in Rome when he was beheaded for his faith.

Sixth, consider James, half-brother to Jesus. There are indications in scriptures that Jesus' siblings thought he was a little off. They weren't seeing Jesus as the Messiah. Later, after the resurrection, we see that James becomes a strong leader in the Jerusalem church. Why the change, James? It's because he saw the resurrected Christ. No longer would James consider Jesus merely a sibling; he would now consider him "Lord and Savior."

Seventh, consider Lazarus, who Jesus raised from the dead. I'll go into more detail on this one because many do not commonly know this story. Jesus was away from Bethany when he heard of Lazarus being sick. He purposely tarried there two days longer before he left to go to Bethany. Upon arriving in Bethany, he was informed that Lazarus had been in the tomb for four days. Jesus, in reality, already knew that Lazarus had died before he had arrived.

Jesus already planned to raise Lazarus from the dead before coming back to Bethany. Martha and Mary greeted him with tears, and Jesus was led to the tomb. Jesus commanded that the stone be moved and then proceeded to call Lazarus out. Lazarus, bound hand and foot with wrappings, came out of the tomb. Lazarus had just been raised from the dead in accordance with what Jesus had planned to do.

I've heard it taught that the Pharisees believed the spirit of man could hover over a body for three days, but after four days, the man's spirit leaves the body for good. No man comes back after being dead for four days. The body decays. This is why I believe Jesus tarried the extra time. He wanted all to know that Lazarus was raised through the power of God. There would be no mistake concerning the presence and power of God in this event.

Many became believers after beholding this event, and rightly so. This clearly was an act of a divine nature. However, have you ever pondered what happened to Lazarus after this event? The scriptures tell us that the chief priests took counsel that they might put Lazarus to death (John 12:10). With that in mind, I was in Larnaca, Cyprus, in 1982, where I visited the Church of St. Lazarus and also followed the first missionary journey of Paul and Barnabas. Tradition tells us that things got hot for Lazarus after he had been raised from the dead. The chief priests wanted to kill him, for he was living proof of the power of God through Jesus. Thus, Lazarus departed the area and proclaimed the gospel in Cyprus, where he eventually died his second death.

This is of keen interest to me. Lazarus returned to life and became on fire for Jesus Christ as he started a ministry in Cyprus. He spread the gospel of Jesus Christ. His priorities in this life were to promote the Lord Jesus and tell others they could have eternal life if they believed in Him. Make no mistake, I'm sure he shared and related his testimony of what Jesus had done for him. I believe Lazarus's priorities were in good order. In light of what he experienced, and actions of his life after he had returned from the dead, are our priorities in good order? Yes, Jesus, resurrected from the tomb. This is not some fable or myth, but reality.

Golgotha's Skull

Chapter 2

Jesus and Golgotha

As a young Christian traveling to different sites in the Bible, including Golgotha, I typically retained my focus on Jesus and how things related to Him in so many ways. As I read my Bible, I could also see how direct and typical prophecy consistently pointed to Jesus from the Old Testament to the New Testament.

Merriam-Webster Dictionary defines prophecy as a prediction of something to come. Direct prophecy will be direct and specific, perhaps giving a name or specific event to occur at a later time. Typical prophecy will be more representative, illustrative or foreshadowing of an event to come. It typically describes as it's correlated to a future event. God uses both approaches to prophecy, especially as seen toward Jesus.

Let me break some of this down in simple analysis. In order to convey some prophetic fulfillments, I'll use the following scriptures to compare in support:

- **John 19:9**—"And went again into the judgment hall, and saith unto Jesus, Whence art thou? **But Jesus gave him no answer.**"

  John 19:16—"Then delivered he him therefore unto them to be crucified. And they took Jesus, **and led him away.**"

  Isaiah 53:7 says, "**Like a lamb he was led to slaughter.** Like a sheep silent before shearers, **he did not open his mouth.**"

- **John 19:14**—"And it was the **preparation of the passover**, and about the sixth hour: and he saith unto the Jews, Behold your King!"

  John 19:32–33—"Then came the soldiers, and brake the legs of the first, and of the other which was crucified with him. But when they came to Jesus, and saw that he was dead already, they brake not his legs."

  Numbers 9:12 says the **bones of the Passover Lamb were not to be broken.** The **Roman soldiers broke the legs of the other two who were crucified with Jesus, "but did not break one bone"** of Jesus. John the Baptist previously identified Jesus as the **Passover Lamb of God** in John 1:29, and Jesus was slain during Passover.

> As I read my Bible, I could also see how direct and typical prophecy consistently pointed to Jesus from the Old Testament to the New Testament.

- **John 19:34**—"But **one of the soldiers with a spear pierced his side**, and forthwith came there out blood and water."

  Zechariah 12:10 says, "**they shall look on him whom they have pierced.**"

- **John 19:38**—"And after this **Joseph of Arimathea**, being a disciple of Jesus, but secretly for fear of the Jews, besought Pilate that he might take away the body of Jesus: and Pilate gave him leave. **He came therefore, and took the body of Jesus.**"

  Isaiah 53:9 says, "**His grave was assigned with wicked men yet with a rich man in his death.**" Joseph of Arimathea was a **rich man** who took the body of Jesus and placed in his tomb.

- **John 19:20**—"This title then read many of the Jews: for **the place where Jesus was crucified was nigh to the city**: and it was written in Hebrew, and Greek, and Latin."

  Exodus 29:14 says that the flesh of the bull and its hide and its refuse shall be burned with fire outside the camp. It was a sin offering. **Jesus was crucified outside the walls of the city**.

  Hebrews 13:12 says that **Jesus gate suffered outside the gate** that He might sanctify the people through His blood. Again, **Jesus was crucified outside the walls of Jerusalem**.

- **John 19:28–29**—"After this, Jesus knowing that all things were now accomplished, that the scripture might be fulfilled, saith, I thirst. Now there was set a vessel full of vinegar: and **they filled a spunge with vinegar**, and put it upon hyssop, and **put it to his mouth.**"

  Psalm 69:21 says, "They gave me also gall for my meat; and in my thirst they gave me vinegar to drink."

- **John 19:23–24**—"Then the soldiers, when they had crucified Jesus, **took his garments, and made four parts, to every soldier**

a part; and also his coat: now the coat was without seam, woven from the top throughout. They said therefore among themselves, **Let us not rend it, but cast lots for it**, whose it shall be: that the scripture might be fulfilled, which saith, They parted my raiment among them, and for my vesture they did cast lots. These things therefore the soldiers did."

Psalm 22:18 says, "They **part my garments among them**, and **cast lots upon my vesture**." We see how the clothing of Jesus was divided by the soldiers, and lots cast for the seamless coat.

- **John 20:12**—"And **seeth two angels in white sitting, the one at the head, and the other at the feet, where the body of Jesus had lain**."

Exodus 25:18 says, "And thou shalt make two cherubims of gold, of beaten work shalt thou make them, in the two ends of the mercy seat." This is significant because on the Day of Atonement, the high priest placed the blood of the sacrifice for the sins of the people on the mercy seat in the Holy of Holies. **Notice that Jesus had been placed between where the two angels were sitting, the supreme sacrifice for the sins of mankind.**

- **John 3:14**—"And as Moses lifted up the serpent in the wilderness, even so must the Son of man be lifted up."

Numbers 21:8—"And the L ORD said unto Moses, Make thee a fiery serpent, and set it upon a pole: and it shall come to pass, that every one that is bitten, **when he looketh upon it, shall live**." **Jesus, in His death, was lifted up in crucifixion. He wasn't stoned in accordance with typical Israelite tradition.**

- **Psalm 22:14–18**—"I am poured out like water, and all my bones are out of joint: my heart is like wax; it is melted in the midst of my bowels. My strength is dried up like a potsherd; and my tongue cleaveth to my jaws; and thou hast brought me into the dust of death. For dogs have compassed me: the assembly of the wicked have inclosed me: they pierced my hands and my feet. I may tell all my bones: they look and stare upon me. They part my garments among them, and cast lots upon my vesture." —These words are describing the pains of crucifixion, depicting the suffering of the Messiah. Crucifixion was an agonizing and horrible death. This means of execution was not known until Roman times, and was used by the Romans against slaves, foreigners, and criminals that were not Roman citizens. The Romans perfected the art of crucifixion, and, of course, Jesus was crucified in accordance with scripture.

- **Luke 24:6–8**—"He is not here, but is risen: remember how he spake unto you when he was yet in Galilee, Saying, **The Son of man must be delivered into the hands of sinful men, and be crucified, and the third day rise again**. And they remembered his words."

Matthew 12:40 says, "For as Jonas was three days and three nights in the whale's belly; so shall the Son of man be three days and three nights in the heart of the earth." **Jesus was prophesying his death and resurrection**, and thus it came to be.

Tyre Hippodrome

Chapter 3

Tyre, Lebanon

While assigned to Observer Group Lebanon (OGL) for UNTSO, I lived in Nahariya, Israel. Nahariya is just south of the Lebanese border by the Mediterranean Sea. Although we lived in Israel, we would go across the Lebanese border and perform duties in southern Lebanon. We had a forward-based office in Tyre, Lebanon, where we would depart from after crossing the border in the performance of our duties. Tyre is a nicely-located area along the Mediterranean Sea. Little did I know the biblical history of this area and the remarkable prophetic fulfillments that would take place over a great span of time. Ezekiel spent his early years in Jerusalem but was taken with other hostages by Nebuchadnezzar to Babylon in 597 B.C. Let me use two passages from the book of Ezekiel as I lay a foundation to explain from.

> **Ezekiel 26:3–9**—"Therefore thus saith the Lord God; Behold, I am against thee, **O Tyrus, and will cause many nations to come up against thee, as the sea causeth his waves to come up. And they shall destroy the walls of Tyrus, and break down her towers: I will also scrape her dust from her, and make her like the top of a rock. It shall be a place for the spreading of nets in the midst of the sea**: for I have spoken it, saith the Lord God: and it shall become a spoil to the nations. And her daughters which are in the field shall be slain by the sword; and they shall know that I am the Lord. **For thus saith the Lord God; Behold, I will bring upon Tyrus Nebuchadrezzar king of Babylon, a king of kings, from the north, with horses, and with chariots, and with horsemen, and companies, and much people. He shall slay with the sword thy daughters in the field: and he shall make a fort against thee, and cast a mount against thee, and lift up the buckler against thee. And he shall set engines of war against thy walls, and with his axes he shall break down thy towers.**"

> **Ezekiel 26:12**—"And they shall make a spoil of thy riches, and make a prey of thy merchandise: and they shall break down thy walls, and destroy thy pleasant houses: and **they shall lay thy stones and thy timber and thy dust in the midst of the water**."

So how did history and archeological evidence fulfill these scriptures? First, Nebuchadnezzar laid siege to Tyre for thirteen years (585–572 B.C.) and eventually destroyed it at the end of the siege. During this siege, he surrounded the city; however, the people of Tyre resettled just offshore to an island during Nebuchadnezzar's time of siege. He knocked things down and left debris, timber, and rubble, but he could not have total victory because the people had built and fortified themselves on this island off shore.[1]

Even though Nebuchadnezzar got the victory, it was not complete in accordance with scripture. Then along comes Alexander the Great in 332 B.C. about 250 years later after Nebuchadnezzar. He had just defeated Darius of the Medes and Persians at the Battle of Isus in 333 B.C. He then besieged the city for six months and finally captured it by building a causeway from the mainland to the island area. He used the debris and rubble that remained on the main area and literally cast it into the sea to build this remarkable causeway.[2]

The causeway was about 2,000 feet long. As his men proceeded to build the causeway, they were being attacked by the Tyrians behind their high and thick walls that they had built. Alexander's men would use their mobile protective shields (called tortoises) to protect themselves from the projectiles coming their way. Once Alexander got to the walls, he used high towers (160 feet high) with drawbridges he had built to get them over the walls when they got there. This was no small feat.[3]

To protect his flanks, Alexander went back to areas he had previously conquered and used them and their ships to come against Tyre in wave after wave. Ships were used from Rhodes, Byblus, Lycia, Cilicia, and other areas.

Some key observations:

- Nebuchadnezzar (by name) did come against Tyre.
- The walls of Tyre were destroyed.
- She was scraped like a barren rock when Alexander threw her debris, timber and rubble into the sea to build the causeway. The remains of the causeway are still there to this day as it was made of stone.

---

[1] The Ryrie Study Bible, NAS, Commentary Notes (Chicago, Illinois: Moody Bible Institute, Copyright 1976, 1978), p. 1264.

[2] Ibid, p. 1263.

[3] Werner Keller, *The Bible as History* (New York, NY: William Morrow and Company, Inc., 1981), pp. 307–308.

- Nations came against her as wave after wave in the sea.
- Tyre shall be a place for the spreading of nets in the midst of the sea. Looking over the Mediterranean Sea, and considering the flatness of the area, this certainly pertains.

On a personal observation, in the interest of trivia, the chariot scenes for the 1959 movie *Ben Hur*, starring Charlton Heston, were filmed in Tyre.

Sphinx of Memphis

Chapter 4

Memphis, Egypt

....

While assigned to Observer Group Egypt (OGE) for UNTSO, I lived in Heliopolis, Egypt (Cairo area). While there, I had the opportunity to visit many fascinating places during my free time. One place I visited was Memphis, Egypt—not Tennessee—and no, Elvis was not there. Visiting Memphis, one could see some huge statues that had been knocked down. The frontal areas seemed to have been well-preserved. Of course, Memphis, like most of Egypt, has a very interesting history.

It was conquered by Cambyses, who was the son of Cyrus the Great and his wife, Cassandane. When Cyrus died in 530 B.C., Cambyses succeeded him. In 525 B.C. Cambyses invaded Egypt. He proceeded to defeat the Egyptians, first in Pelusium, as he marched towards Memphis, the key area in Middle Egypt. The conquest of Egypt was the major achievement of Cambyses' reign.[4] In reference to Pelusium, it was an important city in this march, where the easternmost part of the Nile Delta reached the Mediterranean Sea. To get to Memphis, Cambyses had go through Pelusium. Pelusium was located just southeast of current day Port Said in the Sinai Peninsula.

I remember when I was doing an aerial reconnaissance operation during 2007 when I was attached to the Multinational Force Organization (MFO) in the Sinai. The MFO is a peacekeeping force in the region, and I was serving as a civilian observer in the organization. We flew over this area not far from Port Said, and a more senior civilian observer in the aircraft pointed down to ruins of Pelusium. As we flew over the ruins, my mind raced back to the Battle of Pelusium when Cambyses marched towards Middle Egypt and conquered Memphis.

> Cambyses used trickery to open up the route into Egypt and the path to victory. Little did he know that he was being used to fulfill prophetic words of scripture.

Polyaenus, a second century A.D. Macedonian author, claimed that Cambyses captured Pelusium by using an outstanding and cunning strategy. The Egyptians defended Pelusium with great resolve. As Cambyses advanced, the Egyptians hurled missiles and stones and fire at his forces with great catapults. To counter this barrage, Cambyses placed before his forces dogs, sheep, cats, ibises, and other animals that the Egyptians held sacred. The Egyptians immediately stopped

---

[4] The Editors of Encyclopedia Britannica, "Cambyses II," Encyclopedia Britannica, Inc., April 3, 2020, https://1ref.us/1ak (accessed June 10, 2020).

their operations, out of fear of hurting the animals, which they held in veneration. Cambyses then captured Pelusium, and this opened up the route towards Memphis.[5]

Once Cambyses arrived in Memphis, he knocked their idols down, basically to show that he was greater than their gods. This is most viable after seeing these idols first-hand with well-preserved frontal portions. In other words, sand protected or preserved these face-down frontal features and portions through the annals of time.

I've listed an important scripture below. The idols were destroyed, and fear was generated in Egypt. Cambyses used trickery to open up the route into Egypt and the path to victory. Little did he know that he was being used to fulfill prophetic words of scripture.

> **Ezekiel 30:13**—"Thus saith the Lord God; **I will also destroy the idols, and I will cause their images to cease out of Noph**; and there shall be no more a prince of the land of Egypt: and **I will put a fear in the land of Egypt**." "Memphis" is another name for "Noph."

---

[5] "Polyaenus: Stratagems—Book 7," English Translation (adapted from translation by R. Shepherd, 1793), website: attalus.org, https://1ref.us/1al (accessed Aug. 23, 2020).

Amman Skyline

Chapter 5

Ammon

••

During my assignment with UNTSO, I also spent some time in Amman, Jordan. Living there for a season gave me an appreciation for the history and topography of the land. As one studies the history of Amman, one sees that the Babylonians and nomadic Transjordan tribes came against them from the east. A scripture spoken against Ammon reads as follows:

> **Ezekiel 25:4**—"Behold, therefore **I will deliver thee to the men of the east for a possession**, and **they shall set their palaces in**

thee, and make their dwellings in thee: they shall eat thy fruit, and they shall drink thy milk."

Initially, Nebuchadnezzar and the Babylonians subjugated them about five years after they destroyed Jerusalem, but later in time, they were also subjugated by wandering, nomadic Arab tribes of the desert from the east. It's interesting that God referenced their milk being drank. Milk was a principal sustenance of those people, whose riches consisted chiefly in their stocks of cattle. Nomadic tribes could easily set their dwellings within, as they picked up and moved into another place. Further, the vineyards and fruit of the land were also enjoyed by the conquerors. God's Word was fulfilled in time.[6]

However, it doesn't stop there. I want to reference Jeremiah 49:6 and Jeremiah 48:47. Basically, God says that He was going to restore Ammon and Moab.

> **Jeremiah 49:6**—"And afterward I will bring again the captivity of the children of Ammon, saith the LORD."
>
> **Jeremiah 48:47**—"Yet will I bring again the captivity of Moab in the latter days, saith the LORD. Thus far is the judgment of Moab."

Ammon and Moab basically comprised current day Jordan. Ammon was to the north, and Moab to the south in previous times. God said that He would restore these areas, and, thus, He did. I lived in Amman for about two months. It's a modern city with a modern airport. It has millions of people today. However, if you go back about 100 years ago, you'll see that there was just a handful of people in Amman by comparison. It has greatly increased in population and restoration. Point again, God honors His Word.

---

[6] The Ryrie Study Bible, NAS, Commentary Notes (Chicago, Illinois: Moody Bible Institute, 1976, 1978), p. 1263.

The King's Highway

Chapter 6

Edom

••

An exceptionally interesting place I visited while living in Jordan was Petra. Traveling along the King's Highway from Amman to Petra was outstanding and scenic as well. Petra is located about 150 miles south of Amman. The winding route of the King's Highway was a trade route of vital importance in the ancient Near East, connecting Africa with Mesopotamia. It ran from Egypt across the Sinai Peninsula to Aqaba, then turned northward across Transjordan, to Damascus, and the Euphrates River.[7]

Many groups have used this key highway over the course of history. The Edomites, Moabites, Ammonites, Nabateans, Romans, Christians, and Muslims are included in this list. As one studies its past, one can easily ascertain that the King's Highway has been an important, historical, and well-used thoroughfare throughout the centuries. It's even referred to in the Bible when the Israelites needed use of it in their Exodus journey from Egypt (Numbers 20:17, 21:22).

One may recall seeing the Harrison Ford movie, "Indiana Jones and the Last Crusade" when they traveled by horseback through a winding narrow passageway with towering granite walls skyrocketing upwards on both sides of the canyon, finally opening up onto a spectacular view of a city, with its walls and pillars literally carved into the face of the massive rock cliffs that surrounded the area. For most, that was their first view of Petra.

Petra is commonly considered one of the Seven Wonders of the World. After walking down a narrow, naturally-carved mountain path, one reaches the ancient Nabatean site. For many years hidden from the modern world, it now offers extraordinary views of rock-hewn buildings, carved out of the very mountainside itself, of beautiful rose-stone color. I literally ran throughout Petra during my brief visit looking at different building structures and remains of ruins so that when I finally returned to the entrance, my shirt was completely soaked from perspiration. That said, my journey could have continued and continued as there was so much to explore. It's such a fascinating place.

Petra is surrounded by mountains that form the eastern flank of the Arabah valley that runs from the Dead Sea to the Gulf of Aqaba. The area around Petra has been inhabited for many years throughout time, and the Nabataeans eventually settled there after defeating the Edomites,

---

[7] WIKIPEDIA, "The Free Encyclopedia," "The King's Highway (ancient)," https://1ref.us/1am (accessed Aug. 23, 2020).

Rock City of Petra

raiding their territory from around 550 B.C. to 400 B.C. The Nabataeans were nomadic Arabs who helped make Petra a major and regional trading location.[8,9]

The Edomites are mentioned many times in the Bible but were completely forgotten in secular history until the nineteenth century when references to them were found in Egyptian and Assyrian monuments. Further, archaeologists led by Ezra Ben-Yosef and Tom Levy helped prove the existence of Edom in their research.[10] So what did the Bible have to say about this area? I'll refer to Isaiah 34:5–9 and Jeremiah 49:16 and then elaborate on some points of prophetic fulfillment.

---

[8] WIKIPEDIA, "The Free Encyclopedia," "Petra," https://1ref.us/1an (accessed Aug. 23, 2020).

[9] Angel, Miguel, "Esau's Descendants, The Edomites," Bible 7 Evidence, November 1, 2014, https://1ref.us/1ao (accessed Aug. 23, 2020).

[10] WIKIPEDIA, "The Free Encyclopedia," "Edom," https://1ref.us/1ap (accessed Aug. 23, 2020).

Isaiah 34:5–9—"For **My sword shall be bathed in heaven; Indeed it shall come down on Edom**, And on the people of My curse, for judgment. The sword of the LORD is filled with blood, It is made overflowing with fatness" (NKJV).

Jeremiah 49:16—"Thy terribleness hath deceived thee, and the pride of thine heart, **O thou that dwellest in the clefts of the rock, that holdest the height of the hill: though thou shouldest make thy nest as high as the eagle, I will bring thee down from thence, saith the LORD**."

The Nabateans used the sword against Edom and defeated them. It's interesting that the Edomites helped the Babylonians when Nebuchadnezzar came against Jerusalem in the 597/586 B.C. time frames, and Nebuchadnezzar even rewarded them with a portion of land for all their supportive efforts in the destruction of Jerusalem. Thus, one can see reference to "recompense for the cause of Zion" in Isaiah 34:8.[11]

You'll notice that "Its streams shall be turned to pitch ..." in Isaiah 34:9. How could this be accomplished? The Edomites were practically impregnable from the assault of enemies. There was just one long canyon-like entrance, where a small force of soldiers could protect the city from being taken by a large army. I understood that the Nabateans blocked the channeled flow of water along the carved rock that went to the Edomites. Stopping water flow was a great tactic used by the Nabateans to take this area.

Per Jeremiah 49:16, though Edom lived high in the rocks, God said that He would bring them down. When one gets into Petra, one sees many shelter dwellings built high up into the mountainsides. It's amazing to view these many dwellings as one looks up and then realize what God said would happen to them, even though they made their nests as high as the

---

[11] Eric Parker, "The Disappearance of Edom," South Marion Church of Christ, https://1ref.us/1aq (accessed Aug. 23, 2020).

eagle. It's an amazing view as memories remain with me even today from this exhilarating visit.

The prophets Ezekiel, Joel, Obadiah, and Malachi also spoke words against Edom, and history corroborates what these prophets spoke against this now desolate place came to pass. Why? It's because God fulfills and honors His Word.

Babylon Replica

Chapter 7

Babylon

I have not lived in Iraq; however, I have lived in Jordan, which borders Iraq. Iraq contained Babylon and Nineveh, two pinnacle cities in ancient times. Babylon affected so much in the Middle East that I think it appropriate to address both it and Nineveh in light of prophetic fulfillment. Ruins of Babylon can be found about fifty-nine miles south of Baghdad. Once revered as one of the pinnacle cities of the world, its hanging gardens are now covered in desert sands.

When thinking of Babylon, one must consider Isaiah 13:19–22 and Jeremiah 51:37.

> **Isaiah 13:19–22**—**"And Babylon, the glory of kingdoms, the beauty of the Chaldees' excellency, shall be as when God overthrew Sodom and Gomorrah. It shall never be inhabited, neither shall it be dwelt in from generation to generation: neither shall the Arabian pitch tent there; neither shall the shepherds make their fold there.** But wild beasts of the desert shall lie there; and their houses shall be full of doleful creatures; and owls shall dwell there, and satyrs shall dance there. And the wild beasts of the islands shall cry in their desolate houses, and dragons in their pleasant palaces: and her time is near to come, and her days shall not be prolonged."

> **Jeremiah 51:37** says, "And Babylon shall become heaps, a dwelling place for dragons, an astonishment, and an hissing, without an inhabitant."

Wow, these passages are loaded. The book of Isaiah was written between 740–680 B.C., maybe 150 or more years before Babylon fell in 539 B.C. to Cyrus of the Medes and Persians. The book of Jeremiah was written between 626–586 B.C., again, years before Babylon fell. Babylon was a phenomenally fortified city. How could anyone forecast its fall? Herodotus, the Greek historian, describes the amazing Babylon, along with some of its content and possessions, as follows:[12]

---

[12] Russell, R., "Ancient Babylonia—Nebuchadnezzar's Babylon," Bible History (Maps, History, Archeology), 2020, https://1ref.us/1ar (accessed Aug. 23, 2020).

- In the form of a square, 14 miles on each side, and of enormous magnitude.
- The brick wall was 56 miles long, 300 feet high, 25 feet thick with another wall 75 feet behind the first wall, and the wall extended 35 feet below the ground.
- 250 towers that were 450 feet high.
- A wide and deep moat that encircled the city.
- The Euphrates River also flowed through the middle of the city. Ferry boats and a half-mile long bridge with drawbridges closed at night.
- "Hanging Gardens" (one of the wonders of the ancient world), and water was raised from the river by hydraulic pumps.
- Eight massive gates that led to the inner city and 100 brass gates.
- Streets were paved with stone slabs three feet square.
- The Great Tower (Ziggurat) and fifty-three temples, including the "Great Temple of Marduk." One hundred eighty altars to Ishtar.
- Golden image of Baal and the Golden Table (both weighing over 50,000 lbs. of solid gold).
- Two golden lions, a solid gold human figure (eighteen feet high).
- Nebuchadnezzar's palace was considered to be the most magnificent building ever erected on earth.

During the lifetime of Isaiah, the city of Babylon was utterly destroyed by Sennacherib in the year 689 B.C. Later, when Nebuchadnezzar became king of Babylon, he rebuilt it. Then, upon capturing Babylon in 539 B.C., the Medes and Persians made it their capital. Half a century later, when the city rebelled, Xerxes partly destroyed it. And it was never completely restored. Since the desolation of Babylon in ancient times, the site has not been inhabited.[13] Let me say it this way, Babylon, as a people, as a nation, and as an empire, has ceased to exist or function in any kind of way.

---

[13] BibleAsk Team, "Did the Bible predict Babylon will never be rebuilt?" BibleAsk, 2020, https://1ref.us/1as (accessed Aug. 23, 2020).

The city itself was buried under sand for centuries. It's safe to say that these facts support the prophecies of Isaiah and Jeremiah.

The only way into the city during 539 B.C. was through one of its gates or through the Euphrates River. As such, Cyrus came up with a cunning plan and decided to enter the city via the river. He actually had his men dig and channel off the Euphrates River upstream, so as to divert and lower the water level to the walking of men. Thus, Cyrus and his men walked into Babylon on the river bed and easily took Babylon. The Persian army conquered the outlying areas of the city while the majority of Babylonians at the city center were unaware of the events.[14]

It was during this time that Belshazzar was having a Babylonian national feast within Babylon, thinking he was safe, even though the Medes and Persians were off at a distance. He sensed no threat as his walls were formidable. That's when the fingers of a human hand wrote on the wall and told him that his kingdom was being taken from him, and thus, it happened that evening as the Medes and Persians seized Babylon and Belshazzar perished.

I imagine someone, from a secular perspective, would have a hard time believing Isaiah could forecast the doom of Babylon 100 years before its rise as a great empire in the ancient world. It became the glory of kingdoms; yet, God fulfills His Word. Enter the Medes and Persians to accomplish the task.

---

[14] "Cyrus takes Babylon," Livius, April 20, 2019, https://1ref.us/1at (accessed Aug. 23, 2020).

Assyrian Artwork Found in Nineveh

Chapter 8

Nineveh

••

Since we discussed Babylon, I think it quite appropriate that we also discuss Nineveh as they both were such historically important Mesopotamia cities in ancient times. Nineveh was located about 317 miles from Babylon on the outskirts of Mosul in current-day Iraq, northwest of Baghdad, along the Tigris River.

In 612 B.C., the Medes and Persians laid siege to Nineveh for three months and, in August, finally broke through the defenses and began plundering and burning the city. The major factor in the city's downfall was the Medes, although the Babylonians had joined forces with them.

According to Diodorus Siculus, a Greek historian, Nineveh had 1,500 towers, each of which was 200 feet high. But at the time of the siege, the Tigris River rose up and flooded, and it took out an entire section of the wall of the city. The river did what the enemy could not do; it breached the walls of Nineveh. Then the enemy was able to come in and penetrate the city itself. The breach in the wall was so great that the chariots of the enemy could get in. They opened the canals used for irrigation and thus flooded the palace. At the time this campaign was carried out, the heavy rains in that area caused the Tigris River to reach flood stage.[15]

> **Nahum 2:3–6 tells us, "The shield of his mighty men is made red, the valiant men are in scarlet: the chariots shall be with flaming torches in the day of his preparation**, and the fir trees shall be terribly shaken. **The chariots shall rage in the streets**, they shall justle one against another in the broad ways: they shall seem like torches, they shall run like the lightnings. He shall recount his worthies: they shall stumble in their walk; they shall make haste to the wall thereof, and the defence shall be prepared. **The gates of the rivers shall be opened, and the palace shall be dissolved**."

The Book of Nahum was believed to have been written somewhere between 663–612 B.C. before the fall of Nineveh in 612 B.C. Nahum even tells us the color of the adversaries' uniforms and shields and about their chariots before this attack ever happened.

The Medes and Babylonians made their shields red by painting them or overlaying them with copper. Their tunics were scarlet, and their

---

[15] "Nineveh Floods," Clover Sites, https://1ref.us/1au (accessed Aug. 23, 2020).

chariots flashed with steel because they attached scythes at right angles to the axles.[16] These are amazing predictions with complete accuracies.

History shows that the Tigris River rose and flooded Nineveh, thus, leading to its fall. Archeology has discovered that about 1,200 feet of the wall is missing on the side of the Tigris River. It seems clear that the floodwaters took out a section of the wall. In summation, flooding of the Tigris River was the way in which the enemy was able to enter and take the city.[17]

---

[16] The Ryrie Study Bible, NAS, Commentary Notes (Chicago, Illinois: Moody Bible Institute, 1976, 1978), p. 1394.

[17] "Nineveh Floods," Clover Sites, https://1ref.us/1au (accessed Aug. 23, 2020).

Olive Grove in the Samaria Mountains

Chapter 9

Samaria

. . . .

I remember visiting Samaria, which was an ancient city in Israel. It was the capital of the northern Kingdom of Israel in the ninth and eighth centuries B.C. time period. The ruins of the city are located in the Samaria Mountains of the West Bank, almost six miles to the northwest of Nablus. Under Ahab the city became a center of Baal worship.

2 Kings 17:6 says, "In the ninth year of Hoshea the king of Assyria took Samaria, and **carried Israel away into Assyria, and**

> placed them in Halah and in Habor by the river of Gozan, and in the cities of the Medes."
>
> **2 Kings 17:22–24** further says, "For the children of Israel walked in all the sins of Jeroboam which he did; they departed not from them; Until the L<small>ORD</small> removed Israel out of his sight, as he had said by all his servants the prophets. **So was Israel carried away out of their own land to Assyria unto this day**. And **the king of Assyria brought men from Babylon, and from Cuthah, and from Ava, and from Hamath, and from Sepharvaim, and placed them in the cities of Samaria instead of the children of Israel**: and they possessed Samaria, and dwelt in the cities thereof."

So what happened to Samaria? At the end of 722 B.C., after a three-year siege, Samaria fell at the hands of Sargon II. According to the annals of Sargon II, he deported 27,290 Israelites over to the territory of Persia and placed other people from around his empire into the area of Samaria to populate the region.[18]

Sargon II was considered a biblical myth throughout modern history until the archaeological excavations of the French scholar, Paul Emile Botta. Botta unearthed Sargon's mighty palace at Dur Sharrukin (Khorsabad), just north of Nineveh near the Tigris River. This remarkable discovery had inscriptions on palace walls, which proved many events in history and those mentioned in the Bible.[19]

> **Micah 1:6** says, "Therefore I will make Samaria as an **heap of the field**, and as plantings of a vineyard: and **I will pour down the stones thereof into the valley, and I will discover the foundations thereof**."

---

[18] Russell, R., "The Destruction of Israel—Sargon II," Bible History [Maps, History, Archeology], 2020, https://1ref.us/1av (accessed Aug. 23, 2020).

[19] Ibid.

Alexander the Great also attacked Samaria in 331 B.C. He killed many of the inhabitants and replaced them with Macedonian colonists.[20]

Samaria was situated on a hill of more than 300 feet elevation, isolated on all sides except the east. Thus, when stones and structures were cast down, they went into the valley below as Samaria was on higher ground.

Today, as one looks over the area from the ruins, one views vineyards and olive trees throughout the area.

It appears as a heap of ruins as one views its surroundings. Once again, the veracity of God's Word is backed by history and archeological evidence. If one were able to go back in time and talk to Micah, he would tell you that God fulfills His Word.

> The veracity of God's Word is backed by history and archeological evidence.

---

[20] WIKISOURCE, "The New International Encyclopedia/Samaria," May 2012, https://1ref.us/1aw (accessed Aug. 23, 2020).

Bronze Age Stone Jars

Chapter 10

Jericho

I recall when I first saw Jericho from a short distance how I was impressed with all the banana plants in the area. Somehow, I didn't associate this with the biblical area and story of how the walls came tumbling down. Then I remind myself that was many centuries ago, and of course, now we're in a different era. Thus, let's go back in time, and now reexamine the biblical story.

> **Joshua 6:20** says, "So the people shouted when the priests blew with the trumpets: and it came to pass, when the people heard the sound of the trumpet, and the people shouted with a great

> shout, that **the wall fell down flat, so that the people went up into the city, every man straight before him, and they took the city.**"
>
> **Joshua 6:24** says, "**And they burnt the city with fire, and all that was therein**: only the silver, and the gold, and the vessels of brass and of iron, they put into the treasury of the house of the Lord."

Excavations at Jericho have revealed that this is precisely what happened. At 620 feet below sea level, Jericho was an imposing city, with not one wall, but two: an inner wall and an outer wall. The outer mudbrick wall had been built atop a revetment wall, making it twice as high. Between the two walls was a sloped rampart, with an upper wall encircling the inner city.[21]

When Kathleen Kenyon excavated on the west side of the archeological site, she discovered, "a heavy fill of fallen red bricks piling nearly to the top of the revetment. These probably came from the wall on the summit of the bank." An Italian-Palestinian team found the identical destruction at the southern end of the mound as well.[22]

Archaeologist, Dr. Bryant Wood explains: "Although Kenyon found the revetment wall and the earthen rampart, she did not find the city wall itself on top of the tell (archeological site). But, astoundingly, a heap of fallen red bricks lay outside the revetment wall. These red bricks almost certainly came from the city wall on top of the archeological site or from a mudbrick parapet wall atop the revetment wall, or both, as Kenyon recognized." Amazingly, this pile of red bricks, which went almost to the top of the revetment wall, would have provided a natural siege ramp that would have allowed the Israelites to go "up into the city" just as the Bible describes.[23]

---

[21] Bryan Windle, "Biblical Sites: Three Discoveries at Jericho," Bible Archeology Report, May 25, 2019, https://1ref.us/1ax (accessed Aug. 23, 2020).

[22] Ibid.

[23] Ibid.

One of Kenyon's great discoveries from Jericho was the grain supply. Her team found many jars more than 3,000 years old, which were all full of burned grain. Why is this important? The military strategy of the day was to lay a siege. An army would surround a city, cut off all food and water supplies, and wait for the people to starve. A besieged city typically contains no food at the time of destruction.[24]

Findings showed that many of the jars were still sealed shut, so the city was full of food while it was being destroyed. The jars full of burned grain show that the city had a full supply of food when it was burned, and the defeat of Jericho likely occurred after the beginning of harvest since the city was so well supplied at the time of attack. In other words, much had already been harvested and stored.

These findings support the biblical narrative:[25]

- The city was strongly fortified (Joshua 2:5, 7, 15, 6:5, 20).
- The attack occurred just after harvest time in the spring (Joshua 2:6, 3:15, 5:10).
- The inhabitants had no opportunity to flee with their food (Joshua 6:1).
- The siege was short (Joshua 6:15).
- The walls were leveled, possibly by an earthquake (Joshua 6:20).
- The city was not plundered (Joshua 6:17–18).
- The city was burned (Joshua 6:24).

In summation, archeological evidence, once again, supports God's Word.

---

[24] C. Michael Patton, "Top Ten Biblical Discoveries in Archeology—# 3 Jericho," Credo House, September 20, 2010, https://1ref.us/1ay (accessed Aug. 23, 2020).
[25] Ibid.

Jerusalem

Chapter 11

Israel

....

As I lived and traveled throughout Israel, I was constantly reminded of its historical biblical past. I would see location after location reminding me of its incredible history. Thus, why not look at Israel as a whole entity in reference to words from God.

Deuteronomy 28:64 says, "And **the Lord shall scatter thee among all people, from the one end of the earth even unto the other**; and there thou shalt serve other gods, which neither thou nor thy fathers have known, even wood and stone." **—Written about 1410 B.C.**

Amos 9:14–15 says, "And I will **bring again the captivity of my people of Israel**, and they shall build the waste cities, and inhabit them; and they shall plant vineyards, and drink the wine thereof; they shall also make gardens, and eat the fruit of them. **And I will plant them upon their land**, and they shall no more be pulled up out of their land which I have given them, saith the Lord thy God." **—Written about 750 B.C., Fulfilled in 1948.**

Ezekiel 36:8–10 says, "But ye, O mountains of Israel, **ye shall shoot forth your branches, and yield your fruit to my people of Israel; for they are at hand to come**. For, behold, I am for you, and I will turn unto you, and ye shall be tilled and sown: And I will multiply men upon you, all the house of Israel, even all of it: and **the cities shall be inhabited, and the wastes shall be builded**." **—Written about 593–571 B.C., Fulfilled in 1948.**

Ezekiel 36:24 says, "For I will take you from among the heathen, and **gather you out of all countries, and will bring you into your own land**." **—Written about 593–571 B.C., Fulfilled in 1948.**

Jeremiah 31:10 says, "Hear the word of the Lord, O ye nations, and declare it in the isles afar off, and say, **He that scattered Israel will gather him, and keep him**, as a shepherd doth his flock." **—Written about 626–586 B.C., Fulfilled 1948.**

Isaiah 43:5–6 says, "Fear not: for I am with thee: **I will bring thy seed from the east, and gather thee from the west; I will say to the north, Give up; and to the south, Keep not back: bring my sons from far, and my daughters from the ends of the earth**." **—Written about 740–680 B.C., Fulfilled in 1948.**

Isaiah 66:7–8 says, "Before she travailed, she brought forth; before her pain came, she was delivered of a man child. Who hath heard such a thing? who hath seen such things? Shall the earth be made to bring forth in one day? or **shall a nation be born at once**? for as soon as Zion travailed, she brought forth her children." —**Written about 740–680 B.C., Fulfilled May 14, 1948.**

When Israel became a nation again in 1948, it was a miracle. Who could have envisioned such a thing happening from a natural perspective? Consider the following:[26]

- In 721 B.C., Assyria destroyed the northern kingdom of Israel. They tortured, killed, and exiled many Jews.
- In 586 B.C., Babylon destroyed the southern kingdom of Judah. They killed and exiled many Jews.
- In A.D. 70, Rome killed an estimated 1.1 million Jews and destroyed Jerusalem and the temple.
- In A.D. 135, Rome killed an estimated 580,000 Jews and exiled many others.
- In the 1930s and 1940s, the Nazis killed an estimated six million Jews. The Nazi plan, called the "final solution," was to exterminate all the Jews. I remember visiting Yad Vashem, the World Holocaust Remembrance Center, outside Jerusalem. It certainly reminds one that the Holocaust certainly took place, and of the depravity of man.
- Government and church leaders at times banished the Jews from living in Spain, England, France, Belgium, and Italy.
- During the Crusades, Jewish villages were often destroyed.

The Jews were scattered and persecuted throughout the world; yet, they continued to maintain their identity. What a remarkable feat. Often conquered or exiled ethnic groups would be assimilated into the different

---

[26] "Ten prophecies being fulfilled today," The Refiner's Fire, https://therefinersfire.org/todays_prophecies.htm (accessed Aug. 23, 2020).

cultures; yet, the Jews maintained their identity throughout hundreds of years.

While assigned to UNTSO in Israel, I conducted some liaison in Metulla, Israel, with an Israeli major born in China. God brought Jews back to Israel from all over the globe, from Europe, Russia, Northern Africa, and other locations. In 1948, there were about 600,000 Jews living in Israel; by the end of the 1900s, it was over six million.

Spending some time in Jerusalem, I thought the following scriptures were quite interesting to read. Jerusalem has probably become the world's most visited religious site in these last days. People continually come from numerous nations around the world to visit it.

> **Zechariah 8:22** says, "Yea, **many people and strong nations shall come to seek the Lord of hosts in Jerusalem**, and to pray before the Lord."
>
> **Micah 4:1** says, "But **in the last days it shall come to pass**, that the **mountain of the house of the Lord** shall be established in the top of the mountains, and it shall be exalted above the hills; and **people shall flow unto it**."

As one drives around Israel, one cannot help but to notice the amount of irrigation that takes place. Israel is a major exporter of fresh produce and a world leader in agricultural technologies despite the fact that the geography of the country is not naturally conducive to agriculture. More than half of the land area is desert, and the climate and lack of water resources do not favor farming. Only 20 percent of the land area is naturally arable; yet, Israel has turned the land into a garden.[27] A great amount of fruit and vegetables are exported to Europe and Russia. God foretold what has transpired in regard to this issue. Please refer to the two scriptures below.

---

[27] WIKIPEDIA, "The Free Encyclopedia," "Agriculture in Israel," https://1ref.us/1az (accessed Aug. 23, 2020).

Isaiah 27:6 says, "He shall cause them that come of Jacob to take root: **Israel shall blossom and bud, and fill the face of the world with fruit.**"

Isaiah 51:3 says, "For the LORD shall comfort Zion: he will **comfort all her waste places**; and **he will make her wilderness like Eden**, and **her desert like the garden of the LORD**; joy and gladness shall be found therein, thanksgiving, and the voice of melody."

Bethsaida Ruins

Chapter 12

Chorazin, Capernaum, Bethsaida, Tiberius

Matthew 11:21–23 says, "Woe unto thee, Chorazin! woe unto thee, Bethsaida! for if the **mighty works, which were done in you, had been done in Tyre and Sidon**, they **would have repented** long ago in sackcloth and ashes. But I say unto you, It shall be more tolerable for Tyre and Sidon at the day of judgment, than for you. And thou, **Capernaum, which art exalted unto heaven,**

shalt be brought down to hell: for if the mighty works, which have been done in thee, had been done in Sodom, it would have remained until this day."

Luke 10:13 says, "**Woe unto thee, Chorazin! woe unto thee, Bethsaida!** for if the **mighty works** had been done in Tyre and Sidon, which have been done in you, they had a great while ago **repented**, sitting in sackcloth and ashes."

After looking at this scripture, one will notice that Tiberius is not mentioned. Chorazin, Capernaum, and Bethsaida are mentioned but not Tiberius. I did that for a reason. Now, let me develop this.

Chorazin, Capernaum, and Bethsaida were very prominent and important cities along the northern shore of the Sea of Galilee during the time of Jesus. They were destroyed by an earthquake around the A.D. 400 time frame,[28] but what about Tiberius? Herod Antipas, son of Herod the Great, built Tiberius in 17 B.C., naming it in honor of the Roman emperor Tiberius.[29] Thus, Tiberius existed in the first century. The point is, Jesus spoke doom to Chorazin, Capernaum, and Bethsaida, but not Tiberius. During this particular earthquake, Tiberius remained intact, even though it existed in the same area as the other locations.

> With great revelation, comes great accountability.

One thing is certain. The Lord put a curse on Chorazin, Capernaum, and Bethsaida, and so they remain to this very day as heaps of rubble with hardly anything left standing to show where they were. Never again were they to be rebuilt after the earthquake even though the beautiful scenery in these areas create for most impressive landscapes. On the other hand,

---

[28] Arthur Eedle, "Capernaum, Bethsaida, & Chorazin," Prophetic Telegraph, November 1, 1995, https://1ref.us/1b0 (accessed Aug. 23, 2020).

[29] Golding, Nechama, "Tiberius," Chabad.ORG, Division of Chabad-Lubavitch Media Center, https://1ref.us/1b1 (accessed Aug. 23, 2020).

Tiberius, though destroyed in part during the course of follow-on centuries, has always been rebuilt and has had a continuous record of occupation, even to this day. I even spent a night in Tiberius.

Matthew 11:21–23 and Luke 10:13 give us reasons for the harsh words from Jesus. Many miracles and mighty works were done by Jesus in Chorazin, Capernaum, and Bethsaida. John 1:44 tells us that the apostles Philip, Andrew, and Peter were even from Bethsaida. Thus, even with all the healings, miracles, and deliverances that transpired in these areas, and there were many, it shows in scripture that there was a lack of repentance. With great revelation, comes great accountability. Here's the moral implication of receiving great revelation—**Repent.**

Tomb of Cyrus

Chapter 13

Cyrus

The Hebrew Bible states that Cyrus, of the Medes and Persians, issued the decree of liberation to the Jews. Cyrus's edict for the rebuilding of the temple in Jerusalem marked a great epoch in the history of the Jewish people.[30]

---

[30] WIKIPEDIA, "The Free Encyclopedia," "Cyrus the Great in the Bible," https://1ref.us/1b2 (accessed Aug. 23, 2020).

> **Isaiah 44:28** says, "That saith of **Cyrus, He is my shepherd, and shall perform all my pleasure: even saying to Jerusalem, Thou shalt be built; and to the temple, Thy foundation shall be laid.**"

It's estimated that the Book of Isaiah was written around 740–680 B.C. It's believed that Cyrus was born around 590–580 B.C. This means **Isaiah prophesied that Cyrus would be the one to issue the edict for the rebuilding of the Temple and Jerusalem, perhaps 100–150 years before Cyrus was even born**.

One must notice that God did not miss on the name, but was specific, that it would be "Cyrus" by name. So many other names to choose from, but God said that it would be Cyrus, and so it was.

Ezra further records this event in the Book of Ezra, written about 456–444 B.C. The following scriptures support.

> **Ezra 1:1–4** says, "Now in the first year of Cyrus king of Persia, that the word of the LORD by the mouth of Jeremiah might be fulfilled, the LORD stirred up the spirit of Cyrus king of Persia, that he made a proclamation throughout all his kingdom, and put it also in writing, saying, **Thus saith Cyrus king of Persia, The LORD God of heaven hath given me all the kingdoms of the earth; and he hath charged me to build him an house at Jerusalem, which is in Judah. Who is there among you of all his people? his God be with him, and let him go up to Jerusalem, which is in Judah, and build the house of the LORD God of Israel, (he is the God,) which is in Jerusalem. And whosoever remaineth in any place where he sojourneth, let the men of his place help him with silver, and with gold, and with goods, and with beasts, beside the freewill offering for the house of God that is in Jerusalem.**"
>
> **2 Chronicles 36:22–23**, written about 450–425 B.C., further corroborates this story as follows, "Now in the first year of Cyrus

king of Persia, that the word of the LORD spoken by the mouth of Jeremiah might be accomplished, the LORD stirred up the spirit of Cyrus king of Persia, that he made a proclamation throughout all his kingdom, and put it also in writing, saying, **Thus saith Cyrus king of Persia, All the kingdoms of the earth hath the LORD God of heaven given me; and he hath charged me to build him an house in Jerusalem, which is in Judah. Who is there among you of all his people? The LORD his God be with him, and let him go up.**"

Thus, Cyrus allowed the exiles to return to Judah and build a temple for God in Jerusalem by issuing a decree. Nearly 50,000 Jews traveled from Babylon to Jerusalem (Ezra 2:64). They brought with them silver and gold, as well as other important articles from Solomon's Temple that had been previously looted by Nebuchadnezzar.

Many believed Cyrus was more than a great man who founded an empire. Many believed that he had exemplary qualities hoped for as a ruler in antiquity, including being tolerant, magnanimous, courageous, and daring. Even so, God moved on his heart to accomplish His will and purpose for Jerusalem and Israel and called him forth by name before he was even born.

Solomon's Temple

Chapter 14

King Zedekiah

The Bible is filled with such amazing prophecies and stories. One that falls into both categories is that of King Zedekiah. He was the last king of Judah and was king when Jerusalem and the temple were destroyed by Babylon in 586 B.C., and the majority of the people were carried into exile.

Zedekiah was twenty-one years old when he became king. Zedekiah ruled for eleven years but continued in the evil of his brothers and nephew Jehoiachin (2 Kings 24:18–20). In his ninth year on the throne, Zedekiah rebelled against Nebuchadnezzar, and, as a result, the Babylonians laid siege to Jerusalem. Zedekiah believed in Egypt's help, but it never materialized. In the eleventh year of Zedekiah's reign, Jerusalem fell to Nebuchadnezzar.[31]

Now, let's examine what the prophet Ezekiel prophesied about Zedekiah.

> **Ezekiel 12:13** says, "My net also will I spread upon him, and he shall be taken in my snare: and **I will bring him to Babylon to the land of the Chaldeans; yet shall he not see it, though he shall die there.**"

So, what happened in response to this prophecy?

> **Jeremiah 52:10–11** says, "**And the sons of the king of Babylon slew Zedekiah before his eyes: he slew also all the princes of Judah in Riblah. Then he put out the eyes of Zedekiah; and the king of Babylon bound him in chains, and carried him to Babylon, and put him in prison till the day of his death.**"

> **2 Kings 25:5–7** says, "**And the army of the Chaldees pursued after the king, and overtook him in the plains of Jericho**: and all his army were scattered from him. **So they took the king, and brought him up to the king of Babylon to Riblah; and they gave judgment upon him. And they slew the sons of Zedekiah before his eyes, and put out the eyes of Zedekiah, and bound him with fetters of brass, and carried him to Babylon.**"

Zedekiah fled the city by night during the siege but was captured by the Babylonians. In the assault, the Babylonians broke down the walls of

---

[31] "Who was King Zedekiah in the Bible?" Got Questions Ministries, January 2, 2020, https://1ref.us/1b3 (accessed Aug. 23, 2020).

Jerusalem, burned the temple, and took the temple articles to Babylon with them.

Regarding Riblah, where Zedekiah was initially taken to Nebuchadnezzar, it served as a base of operation for the king. It's located on a broad plain about twenty miles south of Hamath (modern Hama in Syria), on the main road between Egypt and Mesopotamia. The Orontes River flows past the site on the west side.

Thus, Ezekiel's prophecy was fulfilled—**Zedekiah was blinded after seeing his sons killed before his eyes, bound in chains, and taken to Babylon, where he lived all the rest of his days, yet he did not see it, and he died there.** This was such an amazing fulfillment.

God's Law

Chapter 15

Josiah

The story of Josiah is a tremendous revelation of God's fulfillment of scripture. However, let's first give you a little background on Josiah, who would do great works for God. When Josiah was eight years old, he became king of Judah. He tried to do what was right in God's sight, just like King David had done. Now, let's develop this a little bit further.

When Josiah was sixteen, he became a worshipper of God, and when he was twenty, he began removing all the idols from Jerusalem and Judah. He cleansed the land by tearing down all the altars to the false gods and removed the priests who instructed the people to worship them.

When Josiah was twenty-six, after he had cleansed the land, he sent some people to go repair the temple of God. They canvassed the land and received donations for this noble work of temple repair. They took the donations to Hilkiah, the high priest, so that he could pay the workers who were to do the repairs. They did their work faithfully.

As they were working, Hilkiah found the Book of the Law from Moses, and the Book of the Law was subsequently read to Josiah. When Josiah heard the words, he was saddened, and he tore his clothing. He became upset because the people of the land were not doing what they were supposed to do before God.

A prophet was then found. The prophet conveyed that God was not pleased that the people had been worshipping other gods and doing evil before Him. But because Josiah had a tender and humble heart, and had been disheartened about all the things the people were doing wrong, God said he would not bring disaster to the land while Josiah was still alive. So they came and told Josiah everything the prophet said.

> God had the name right **300** years later when **Josiah** accomplished this mighty task.

Then Josiah gathered everyone in Judah together and read to them the Book of the Law that had been found in the temple. The king then made a promise to God to walk in His ways and keep His commandments with all his heart and all His soul. And he asked all to promise as well.[32]

With that said, let's examine an important scripture concerning Josiah from the first book of Kings.

> **1 Kings 13:2** says, "And he cried against the altar in the word of the Lord, and said, O altar, altar, thus saith the Lord; **Behold,**

---

[32] Jason Arsenault, "The Story of Josiah," Bible Stories, October 10, 2011, https://1ref.us/1b4 (accessed Aug. 23, 2020).

> **a child shall be born unto the house of David, Josiah by name; and upon thee shall he offer the priests of the high places that burn incense upon thee, and men's bones shall be burnt upon thee."**

This astonishing prediction, specifically naming Josiah, was fulfilled about 300 years later in the second book of Kings.[33]

> **2 Kings 23:16** says, "And as **Josiah** turned himself, he spied the sepulchres that were there in the mount, and sent, and **took the bones out of the sepulchres, and burned them upon the altar, and polluted it, according to the word of the LORD which the man of God proclaimed**, who proclaimed these words."

> **2 Kings 23:20** says, "And **he slew all the priests of the high places that were there upon the altars, and burned men's bones upon them**, and returned to Jerusalem."

Josiah ransacked the sepulchers of idolatrous priests and burned the bones on the heathen altars before demolishing them in accordance with 1 Kings 13:2.[34] God had the name right **300** years later when **Josiah** accomplished this mighty task. Just an amazing prophetic fulfillment.

---

[33] The Ryrie Study Bible, NAS, Commentary Notes (Chicago, Illinois: Moody Bible Institute, 1976, 1978), p. 531.

[34] The Ryrie Study Bible, NAS, Commentary Notes (Chicago, Illinois: Moody Bible Institute, 1976, 1978), p. 593.

Section Two—Archeological Evidence

Moses and the Opening of the Red Sea

Chapter 16

Mount Sinai

I was assigned to the MFO in the Sinai as a civilian observer during 2007. I lived at North Camp and traveled extensively throughout the Sinai Peninsula in the performance of my duties during this period.

Some believe that Mount Sinai, traditionally known as Jebel Musa in Arabic, is the mountain where Moses received the Ten Commandments. It's located in the southern part of the Sinai Peninsula. It's a moderately high mountain, 7,497 feet above sea level, near the city of Saint Catherine. Immediately north of the mountain is the sixth century Saint Catherine's

Monastery. I stayed in the Saint Catherine's area a number of times and even climbed a good section of this rugged mountain. That said, personally, I don't believe this is the true mountain where Moses received the Ten Commandments, even though Helena, the mother of Constantine, proclaimed it to be so.

I do, however, believe that it may be Jebel el-Lawz. It's located in northwest Saudi Arabia, near the Jordanian border, above the Gulf of Aqaba at 8,460 feet above sea level. The name means "Mountain of Almonds" in Arabic. When Moses first left Egypt, he went to Midian.

> **Exodus 2:15** says, "Now when Pharaoh heard this thing, he sought to slay Moses. **But Moses fled from the face of Pharaoh, and dwelt in the land of Midian**: and he sat down by a well."
> —Moses fled to Midian.
>
> **Acts 7:29–30 says,** "Then, at this saying, **Moses fled and became a dweller in the land of Midian**, where he had two sons. **And when forty years had passed, an Angel of the Lord appeared to him in a flame of fire in a bush, in the wilderness of Mount Sinai**" (NKJV). —Moses fled to Midian and spent forty years there.

William G. Dever, an American archeologist specializing in the history of Israel and the Near East in biblical times, states that biblical Midian was in the "northwest Arabian Peninsula, on the east shore of the Gulf of Aqaba on the Red Sea," an area which he notes was "never extensively settled until the 8th.–7th. century B.C."[35] This area now corresponds to a section of current-day Saudi Arabia.

According to the Genesis 25:1–2, the Midianites were the descendants of Midian, who was a son of Abraham and his wife, Keturah. Abraham married Keturah after the death of first wife, Sarah.

---

[35] W.G. Dever, "Who Were the Israelites and Where Did They Come From?", (Grand Rapids, Michigan: William B. Eerdmans Publishing Co., 2006), p. 34.

Exodus 3:1–2 says, "Now **Moses was tending the flock of Jethro his father-in-law, the priest of Midian**. And he led the flock to the back of the desert, and **came to Horeb, the mountain of God. And the Angel of the Lord appeared to him in a flame of fire from the midst of a bush**. So he looked, and behold, the bush was burning with fire, but the bush was not consumed" (NKJV). —Mt. Horeb and Mt. Sinai are used interchangeably in Exodus.

Exodus 3:11–12 says, "But Moses said to God, 'Who am I that I should go to Pharaoh, and that I should bring the children of Israel out of Egypt?' So He said, 'I will certainly be with you. **And this shall be a sign to you that I have sent you: When you have brought the people out of Egypt, you shall serve God on this mountain**'" (NKJV). —Moses would bring the Israelites back to this mountain.

Based on scriptural support, it appears clearly that Mt. Sinai was in Midian, and Midian was in current day Saudi Arabia. I think the following information is now worth consideration.

Exodus 19:18 says, "And **mount Sinai was altogether on a smoke, because the Lord descended upon it in fire: and the smoke thereof ascended as the smoke of a furnace, and the whole mount quaked greatly**." —Jebel el-Lawz has a blackened peak, which sticks out from surrounding mountains. The rocks look as if they've been torched.

Chariot parts were found by Ron Wyatt in 1978 in the Gulf of Aqaba just off the Sinai shore.[36] The biblical account tells us how the people arrived at Mt. Sinai after they crossed the Red Sea. Since the Gulf of Aqaba separates the Sinai Peninsula and Saudi Arabia, it would appear

---

[36] Wyatt Archeological Research, Cornersville, TN., https://1ref.us/1b5 (accessed Aug. 23, 2020).

that this would be the crossing site. Extraordinary underwater film coverage presented through the ministry of Michael Rood actually shows coral-encrusted remains of Pharaoh's chariots and army strewn across the floor of the Red Sea off Nuweiba, leading to Saudi Arabia. I once attended one of his presentations and was exceptionally impressed with the film footage. The photography of the finds was amazing. Fossilized human and horse bones have also been recovered in this stretch of water.

I've visited Nuweiba on several occasions. From Nuweiba one can clearly view a stretch of water over the Gulf of Aqaba to Saudi Arabia. Apparently, there's an underwater land bridge directly from Nuweiba to Saudi Arabia that has a gentle slope both up and down of six degrees. The underwater land bridge is estimated to be about six-tenths of a mile wide (900 m.) by eight miles (13 km.) long between Nuweiba and Saudi Arabia. At the deepest point, the underwater land bridge is estimated to be around 1,000 feet (300 m.) deep. On each side of this underwater land bridge, the water in the Gulf of Aqaba goes dramatically down to about 5,000 feet deep (1,500 m.) for most of its length with a steep forty-five-degree slope to the bottom, not conducive to easily walking up and down with animals.[37]

> **Exodus 14:21–22** says, "And Moses stretched out his hand over the sea; and the LORD **caused the sea to go back by a strong east wind all that night, and made the sea dry land, and the waters were divided. And the children of Israel went into the midst of the sea upon the dry ground: and the waters were a wall unto them on their right hand, and on their left.**"
>
> **Exodus 15:8** says, "And with the blast of thy nostrils the **waters were gathered together, the floods stood upright as an heap, and the depths were congealed in the heart of the sea.**"

---

[37]"Red Sea Crossing Site Rediscovered," BiblePlus, https://1ref.us/1b6 (accessed Aug. 23, 2020).

Merriam-Webster defines "Congeal" as—to change from a fluid to a solid state by, or as if by cold. I'm not totally sure how God did this miracle, but it appears that He stood the waters up on both sides in the divide, creating a channel and froze both walls of water with a cold east wind before letting them melt down over the Egyptians.

This, I know: it's hard to dispute the coral-encrusted chariot wheels and all the other associated artifacts found in this stretch of water.

The historical significance of the Nuweiba site as that of the Exodus crossing was apparently known in ancient times as well. This is attested to by the discovery of "commemorative columns with inscriptions erected by King Solomon" on both the Sinai and Saudi Arabian sides of the crossing. The Hebrew words Mizram (Egypt), death, water, pharaoh, Edom, Yahweh, and Solomon were intact on one of the columns. Apparently, one can conclude King Solomon had these columns erected 400 years after the miracle of the crossing of the Red Sea on dry land.[38] On the Egyptian side, one of these red granite columns can be seen standing in place in the Nuweiba area.

Moses and the Israelites probably traveled down Wadi Watir into Nuweiba. Wadi Watir is a narrow, winding wadi with some occasional date palms and acacia trees. It's the most direct route between Nuweiba and the main inland road cutting across the Sinai. This narrow canyon is surrounded by exceptionally rugged mountainous rock.

It's easy to understand how Pharaoh thought that he had Moses and the Israelites trapped against the sea after they traveled down this winding passage leading into Nuweiba Beach. You see, from the northern direction of Nuweiba was an Egyptian fortress whose ruins still stand as evidence of Egyptian strategic interest. This would have prevented them from going north after they entered the beach area. I can imagine how this may have looked for Pharaoh from a military and tactical perspective because I've traveled Wadi Watir several times.

---

[38] "The Red Sea Crossing," Ark Discovery International, ArkDiscovery.com, https://1ref.us/1b7 (accessed Aug. 23, 2020).

Pharaoh thought that he had Moses and the Israelites pinned in, but God had other thoughts on how He was going to handle this situation. Exodus 14:3 says that the wilderness had shut them in. This is further corroborated from the writings of first-century Jewish historian Titus Flavius Josephus (*Antiquities of the Jews*, Book II, Chapter 15) when he clarified that the crossing point was mountainous, which would have trapped the Israelites in on three sides.

Wadi Watir is an amazing route to travel with its winding turns, steep change of elevation, and rugged mountainous scenery, leading into Nuweiba. It's also worth mentioning that Nuweiba lies on a large flood plain measuring about fifteen square miles. It would have had to have been a good-sized area to accommodate the size of the Israelite group. Looking westward from the Nuweiba Beach area, one can easily see how the mountains surround and press towards Nuweiba in an embracing, surrounding, and picturesque view.

In reference to Jebel el-Lawz, Ron Wyatt and others have visited the mountain itself. Some observations that are apparent in the area:[39,40]

- Petroglyphs of the Egyptian cow and bull gods, which seem to identify the altar of the golden calf.
- Sacrificial altar near the original tabernacle site.
- Remnants of twelve stone pillars can also be found at the base of mountain.
- Remnants of the uncut stone altar where the priests sacrificed animals unto the Lord at the base of the mountain.
- Huge split rock that could have been the site where millions of gallons of water gushed into the thirsty Israelite camp.

---

[39] "The Real Mt. Sinai Is In Saudi Arabia!," Discovery World (A Publication of Significant Archeological Discoveries and Biblical Truths), https://1ref.us/1b8 (accessed Aug. 23, 2020).

[40] "Jebel el Lawz—Right Mount Sinai, archeological findings," AmazingHope.net, https://1ref.us/1b9 (accessed Aug. 23, 2020).

- Footprints carved in rocks at base and around mountain area.
- Cave where Elijah could have stayed during his sojourn to the mountain.

As Ron Wyatt brought attention to Jebel el-Lawz in 1984, Saudi Arabian authorities surrounded the mountain area with fencing, placed a guardhouse to watch for trespassers, declared the area an archeological site, and closed it off to people.

Based on my visit to Jebel Musa in St. Catherine, I saw nothing in comparison to what's said to be at Jebel el-Lawz. That said, I wanted to visit Jebel el-Lawz during the course of my time while I was assigned to the MFO during 2007 and early 2008; however, I was not able to make the visit. Certain restrictions exist within Saudi Arabia. I had hoped to team up with an individual who might have had the connections to get us in, but it never materialized. Even so, we probably would have had to camp out and use binoculars because of the fencing and guard situation that would have been present at the mountain.

Is Jebel el-Lawz the real Mt. Sinai? I know that others disagree, but in my opinion, it certainly appears to be hard to dismiss based on the archeological evidence and artifacts that support.

Mount Ararat

Chapter 17

Noah's Ark

Mount Ararat is a snow-capped and dormant compound volcano in the extreme east of Turkey. It consists of two major volcanic cones: Greater Ararat and Little Ararat. Greater Ararat is the highest peak in Turkey and the Armenian Highland with an elevation of 5,137 m. (16,854 ft.); Little Ararat's elevation is 3,896 m. (12,782 ft.).[41]

---

[41] WIKIPEDIA, "The Free Encyclopedia," "Mount Ararat," https://1ref.us/1ba (accessed Aug. 24, 2020).

Many Christians believe that Mt. Ararat in Turkey is the final resting place of Noah's ark, which the Bible says protected Noah, his family, and pairs of every animal species on earth during a divine deluge that wiped out most of humanity. I've been to Turkey, but I never visited Mt. Ararat.

> **Genesis 8:4** says, "And **the ark rested in the seventh month, on the seventeenth day of the month, upon the mountains of Ararat.**"

> Ron Wyatt claimed to have found multiple artifacts evidence of pre-flood metal production, anchor stones, tombstones with pertinent inscriptions, associated housing structures, giant altar and complex, and a boat-like object with measurements exceptionally comparable to the dimensions of Noah's ark.

A 1993 CBS program, "*The Incredible Discovery of Noah's Ark*," featured Fernand Navarra, a Frenchman explorer, who reported he found a wooden beam in a crevasse on Ararat and saw a large, dark object under the ice in 1955. Navarra's son shot black-and-white film footage of his father carrying the beam down from the Ahora Gorge area. I know when I viewed this program that I was pretty impressed. However, some analysts have since disputed some of the findings from members of the expedition. For example, in regards to the testimony of Fernand Navarra and his ark-like wood, according to some, it was ultimately found to be far less in age—and some of Navarra's expedition team members claim he purchased it from a Turkish village.[42]

---

[42] Jim Lippard, "Sun Goes Down in Flames: The Jammal Ark Hoax," *Skeptic*, vol. 2, no. 3, 1993, pp. 22–33.

In regard to another location on the mountains of Ararat, earthquakes and heavy rain exposed a large ark-shaped formation in 1948. The site, named Durupinar, was designated a national park in Turkey and is easier to get to than the other ark location. Ron Wyatt claimed to have found multiple artifacts in this area to bolster his assertion that the object is indeed the ark. Artifacts included: evidence of pre-flood metal production, anchor stones, tombstones with pertinent inscriptions, associated housing structures, giant altar and complex, and a boat-like object with measurements exceptionally comparable to the dimensions of Noah's ark.[43,44] There seems to be a lot to support the validity of this site.

Even so, some have disputed Wyatt's findings at this location.

Did Ron Wyatt find the resting place of Noah's Ark? Possibly, and one can also look at this way. Even those who saw Christ perform miracles with their own eyes crucified Him. Some people will never believe "even if one came back from the dead."

One thing we know for sure from God's Word: Noah's ark landed on the mountains of Ararat.

For those who believe that the flood never took place, or was just a myth, I submit to you that many nationalities have recorded histories of a "Great Flood" that destroyed mankind except for one family that survived. This remarkable event was impressed into the memories and recollections of ancestors in all races.

In 1872 tablet accounts from the Library of Assur-banipal at Nineveh were discovered by English Assyriologist George Smith that described the flood similar to the biblical storyline. These tablet accounts had been copied from tablets dating back before Abraham. Smith actually achieved great fame by his translation of the Chaldean account of the

---

[43] "The Search for Noah's Ark, part 2," Ark Discovery International, ArkDiscovery.com, https://1ref.us/1bb (accessed Aug. 24, 2020).

[44] Wyatt Archeological Research, Cornersville, TN., https://1ref.us/1bc (accessed Aug. 24, 2020).

Ark Dig Site, Mount Ararat

"Great Flood," which he read before the Society of Biblical Archeology during the same year. Other nations have similar flood accounts.

Did a "Great Flood" occur during the history of mankind? Oh, yes, the flood occurred. God foretold it, and it was fulfilled during the time of Noah.

Jerash Ruins

Chapter 18

Damascus

....

While I was living and working in Amman, Jordan, during my assignment with UNTSO, I had the opportunity to go to Damascus, Syria, for a short visit. Damascus is about 120 miles north of Amman. The trip took me close to four hours via vehicle. One has to cross the border and process through immigration procedures.

I remember when driving north to Damascus that I visited the ruins of Jerash, a once-exceptionally-developed Roman city. The Jerash ruins, about thirty miles north of Amman, are said by some to be the best-preserved Roman ruins outside of Italy. Jerash probably is the second largest tourist attraction in Jordan after Petra.

When I was in Damascus, I was able to visit the walled area where Saul of Tarsus (later to be called Paul) was lifted down in a basket to enable his escape. Some of the structure remains in place. The following scripture pertains:

> **Acts 9:23–25**—"And after that many days were fulfilled, the Jews took counsel to kill him: But their laying await was known of Saul. And they watched the gates day and night to kill him. **Then the disciples took him by night, and let him down by the wall in a basket.**"

Remains of the walls and walled area show where this event in scripture took place. Archeological preservation supports scripture.

This is a side lesson that I learned while on this trip. It doesn't pertain to the subject at hand, but it made a distinct impression on me on how I was to consider or view political news coverage in the future.

While there, I had a conversation with an U.S. Army major serving in that area. He conveyed to me how he got on a bus with some Syrians holding anti-America placards. These Syrians, apparently for slight compensation, were purposely being transported by the Syrian government to protest at a certain location against America. It was a staged demonstration, where the cameras would film certain scenes and make certain points.

I learned something that day. Staged demonstrations, coupled with appropriate media coverage and spin, creates for propaganda dissemination. Demonstrations can be useful political tools to influence and deceive the masses.

Mount of Sodom with "Lot's Wife" Pillar Rock Formation

Chapter 19

Sodom and Gomorrah

● ●

The names "Sodom and Gomorrah" are commonly linked in today's society. Their reputation as centers of wickedness has lasted down through the centuries and even the word "sodomy" has taken its place in the English language as a legal term for unnatural sex acts. To many people, Sodom and Gomorrah are places from the legendary past, more mythical than real. Sodom was about thirteen miles south of Gomorrah.

Gomorrah was located at the base of Masada. They existed about 4,000 years ago.[45] Even so, they existed in accordance with scripture.

> **Genesis 13:13** says, "But the **men of Sodom were wicked and sinners before the Lord exceedingly**."
>
> **Genesis 19:24** says, "Then the Lord **rained upon Sodom and upon Gomorrah brimstone and fire from the Lord out of heaven**."
>
> **Genesis 19:28** says, "And he looked toward **Sodom and Gomorrah, and toward all the land of the plain, and beheld, and, lo, the smoke of the country went up as the smoke of a furnace**."

Sodom and Gomorrah were situated at the south end of the Dead Sea along a rift, a major plate boundary. At the southwest corner of the Dead Sea is a mountain, largely of crystalline salt, five miles long and over 700 feet high. Its name is Jebel Usdum which, in Arabic, means "Mount of Sodom."[46] Deposits of sulfur in the form of fine sulfur dust pressed into balls, encased and burned around the ring and embedded in ash were found at these sites. Evidence of heat exceeding 3,632 degrees Fahrenheit can be seen in the rock strata and ruins throughout the cities. The amount of ash, charcoal, and calcium sulfate found in these areas confirm overwhelming evidence of extreme heat in these cities.[47,48]

At God's command the rift ruptured, spewing great quantities of liquid and gaseous hydrocarbons high into the atmosphere. These ignited, setting the whole region ablaze and covering it with "fire and brimstone."

---

[45] "Sodom & Gomorrah: Example of Judgment," Holy Land Site, https://1ref.us/1bd (accessed Aug. 24, 2020).

[46] Wood, Bryant, "Have Sodom And Gomorrah Been Found?" *Bible and Spade*, BSP 03:3, 1974, p. 65, https://1ref.us/1be (accessed Aug. 24, 2020).

[47] "Sodom and Gomorrah—a unique layered ash and sulfur," AmazingHope.net, https://1ref.us/1bf (accessed Aug. 24, 2020).

[48] "Sodom & Gomorrah: Example of Judgment," Holy Land Site, https://1ref.us/1bd (accessed Aug. 24, 2020).

Abraham saw the conflagration from Mamre, about twenty miles away. Archeologists further have discovered around 1.5 million bodies in graves in these areas around Sodom and Gomorrah.[49,50]

Biblical archaeologist Dr. Bryant Wood of Associates for Biblical Research located city gates, crushed graves, towers, a temple, the water supply, and thick city walls. Uninhabitable since the destruction, the remains were identified by Dr. Wood as Sodom and Gomorrah. Creation geologist Dr. Steve Austin studied the geological evidence, including the fault zone, the burn layer, the bitumen that erupted, and the city's calamitous fall to its ruin.[51] This certainly seems to confirm the Genesis account.

Evidence shows Sodom and Gomorrah were destroyed with fire and brimstone. Once again, **God's Word is shown to be accurate**.

The Dead Sea, for those not familiar with it, is a large salt lake east of the Judean desert. It's one of the saltiest water bodies in the world at 34 percent and about 420 meters below sea level.[52] I challenge anyone to sink in the Dead Sea. One floats like a cork. I personally tried to sink when I was swimming in it, and could not succeed because of its heavy salt content. I remember running in the Dead Sea Half Marathon during February 2007. At the halfway point, I looked to my right, and there was Masada off at a distance. It's definitely an arid and dry area.

---

[49] Morris, John D. PH.D., "Have Sodom and Gomorrah Been Discovered?" Institute for Creation Research, March 29, 2013, https://1ref.us/1bg (accessed Aug. 24, 2020).

[50] "Sodom & Gomorrah: Example of Judgment," Holy Land Site, https://1ref.us/1bd (accessed Aug. 24, 2020).

[51] Morris, John D. PH.D., "Have Sodom and Gomorrah Been Discovered?" Institute for Creation Research, March 29, 2013, https://1ref.us/1bg (accessed Aug. 24, 2020).

[52] "Dead Sea." BibleWalks.com, https://1ref.us/1bh (accessed Aug. 24, 2020).

Canaanite City Gate, Megiddo

Chapter 20

Hazor, Megiddo, Shiloh

I remember driving along a road in Israel when I saw a sign pointing towards the remains of Hazor. My mind flashed thoughts before me as I pondered where I had seen that name in the Bible. Ah, that was one of the Canaanite cities that Joshua and the Israelites had conquered when they came into the Promised Land.

Joshua 11:10–11 says, "And **Joshua at that time turned back**, and **took Hazor**, and smote the king thereof with the sword: for

Hazor beforetime was the head of all those kingdoms. **And they smote all the souls that were therein with the edge of the sword, utterly destroying them**: there was not any left to breathe: and he **burnt Hazor with fire**."

Hazor remains a very large archaeological site in northern Israel, featuring an upper city area of thirty acres and a lower city area of more than seventy-five acres.[53] Excavations include an acropolis, fortifications, a citadel, storage facilities, houses, stables, a water system of great engineering feat, and many artifacts, including statues, jewelry, and even Egyptian artifacts. The archaeological evidence has shown that a violent fire destroyed the palace around the thirteenth century B.C. period. The fire was so intense with temperatures exceeding 2,300 degrees Fahrenheit that it completely melted clay vessels and the mud bricks that the walls were made of. The combination of large quantities of wood used for the building and olive oil stored in rooms, as well as strong winds, were responsible for such destruction. Evidence strongly supports Joshua and the Israelites setting the fire.[54]

> Hazor remains a very large archaeological site in northern Israel.

Megiddo is about twenty-one miles southeast of Haifa, at the southern end of the lush Jezreel Valley. It was destroyed and rebuilt many times during its tumultuous history, and it was occupied almost continuously for many prior centuries to about 500 B.C. Megiddo has been the site of legendary and key battles throughout time. The "king of Megiddo" was among those Joshua conquered after the Israelites entered the Promised Land in the fourteenth century. The Bible forecasts Armageddon (from the ancient Greek Harmagedon, or Mountain of Megiddo) as the scene of

---

[53] WIKIPEDIA, "The Free Encyclopedia," "Tel Hazor," https://1ref.us/1bi (accessed Aug. 24, 2020).

[54] Black, John, "Joshua and the destruction of Hazor: From myth to reality," Ancient Origins, July 9, 2013, https://1ref.us/1bj (accessed Aug. 24, 2020).

the climactic battle between good and evil. The name has become a serious byword for the end of the world.[55]

> **Joshua 12:20–22** says, "The king of Shimronmeron, one; the king of Achshaph, one; The king of Taanach, one; **the king of Megiddo**, one; The king of Kedesh, one; the king of Jokneam of Carmel, one;"—Among others, these were some of the kings Joshua conquered when he entered the Promised Land.
>
> **Revelation 16:16** says, "And **he gathered them together into a place called in the Hebrew tongue Armageddon**."

As I was driving from Megiddo to Nazareth, I made it a point to stop and get out of my car en route, and look up the beautiful, green lush "Valley of Jezreel." I then began to envision how the armies of the world will, in time, meet on this picturesque valley in the Battle of Armageddon.

Excavation highlights of Megiddo include well-preserved stone steps from around the seventh century B.C.; a Canaanite city gate from 1550–1200 B.C. period; a massive stone wall, about six-and-one-half feet thick, marking the site of a Canaanite palace destroyed in the twelfth century B.C.; two elongated complexes often called Solomon's stables; a "high place" with remains of several Canaanite temples and a circular altar of unhewn stones; a huge circular silo capable of storing a great amount of grain; an impressive underground tunnel to spring water; and a trove of ivory artifacts. Megiddo appears to be a popular visit location for Christian Evangelical Holy Land tours because of its past, but also what's foretold of its future.[56]

Shiloh, another interesting location, is located in the West Bank area and about ten miles north of Bethel. It was established by Joshua, approximately 3,500 years ago, as the spiritual capital of Israel. It was actually the "major Israelite center" before the first temple was built in Jerusalem.

---

[55] "Megiddo," seetheholyland.net, 2020, https://1ref.us/1bk (accessed Aug. 24, 2020).
[56] Ibid.

The tabernacle was placed there, and Israelites from all over the land came to worship at this location. According to Talmudic sources, the ark of the covenant remained at Shiloh for 369 years until it was taken into the battle camp at Ebenezer (1 Samuel 4:3–5) and captured by the Philistines (1 Samuel 4:1, 10–11) near Aphek.[57]

> **Joshua 18:1** says, "And the **whole congregation of the children of Israel assembled together at Shiloh, and set up the tabernacle of the congregation there**. And the land was subdued before them."

When I visited Shiloh, I processed how the tabernacle and ark of the covenant were set up there by the Israelites, and how the great prophet Samuel and others walked the soil. This is where Hannah offered her famous prayer unto God before she conceived Samuel. It was just impressive for me to be there. A sense of awe came over me as I pondered its history when I walked there. Excavations support this as the actual location of Shiloh, and discovered artifacts reflect the different people habitation periods over time.

I've grouped Hazor, Megiddo, and Shiloh together in this section. In each case, they support biblical records. I've given just a little insight into them, but if you care to examine each one of these areas in greater detail and the scriptures, you'll find they support the validity of the Bible.

One can go throughout Israel and regularly visit other biblical sites: Jerusalem, Caesarea, Sea of Galilee, Jordan River, Nazareth, Bethlehem, Beersheba, and numerous other locations. Again, and again, you'll find that archeological and historical evidence supports the Bible.

---

[57] WIKIPEDIA, "The Free Encyclopedia," "Shiloh (biblical city)," https://1ref.us/1bl (accessed Aug. 24, 2020).

Dead Sea Scrolls found in the Qumran Caves

Chapter 21

Dead Sea Scrolls

The Dead Sea Scrolls, discovered in the caves of Qumran near the Dead Sea in 1947, are one of the great archaeological finds in modern-day history. The scrolls, their teachings, the community that created them, their significance for understanding the Hebrew Bible, and the world from which Christianity came forth attest to the importance of their revelations. I still remember visiting the Shrine of the Book in Jerusalem where I viewed a complete manuscript of the Book of Isaiah.

These scrolls (972 in number) were written in Hebrew, Aramaic, and Greek. Many were written centuries apart and had different authors, but they contextually agreed with one another. They were found, ironically, one year before the modern nation of Israel was founded in 1948. These scrolls were hidden by the Essenes, a now-extinct sect of the Jewish nation, for the purpose of preserving them. These scrolls were protected in sealed clay vessels and written on parchment, papyrus, and even copper scrolls.[58]

So why are these findings really significant? The following pertains:

- They support the veracity or truthfulness of the Bible. There were more than forty authors who wrote sixty-six books in three languages, yet the margin of error was minimal. Most of these errors consisted of minor spelling and punctuation differences and did not affect the context of the books. Jesus quoted from the Old Testament, and His quotes match these accounts.[59]
- One of the reasons that the Dead Sea Scrolls are so important to the Christian is that they support what has been recorded in the New Testament.

What does this mean to the Christian? Some of the manuscripts dated back to around 200 B.C. Thus, it meant that God preserved His Word. What one reads today could have been read years before Christ. In natural conclusion, it shows us that the story of the fall, restoration, and redemption of human beings who believe in Jesus Christ as Lord and Savior can also be believed.

---

[58] Wellman, Jack, "What Are the Dead Sea Scrolls? The Reasons They Are Important," What Christians Want to Know (Topics to Equip, Encourage & Energize), May 23, 2018, https://1ref.us/1bm (accessed Aug. 24, 2020).

[59] Ibid.

Section Three—Science and Common Sense Reasoning

Fossilized Fish

Chapter 22

Evolution versus Creationism

History and archeological evidence consistently support the Bible. Yet, many refute the existence of God and follow the teachings of evolution as a way to explain mankind and his development through the ages. Creationism is refuted.

I'm somewhat amazed at how evolutionists do not want to acknowledge the existence of a Creator. Look at all the inventions man has created through his intelligent mind. Can an automobile just appear? No, a series of procedures and systems were specifically designed and put into effect to give the desired results.

The list of inventions goes on and on as one acknowledges man's advancement in this modern age. Yet, man is surrounded by a series of systems and scientific laws around him that continually work together in a cohesive manner and balance. Notice how man's blood system is far more complex than anything man has ever created. Can one get this kind of order out of chaos? Based on common sense alone, I think not.

Just because evolution is taught as fact in many circles doesn't make it so. Tell a lie often enough, and people begin to believe it. Multitudes have been deceived throughout time through the use of misguided, inaccurate, or just plain deceitful information. Corrupt leaders know this approach all so well, as history has shown us. Many corrupt leaders, over time, have used inaccurate information and lies to lead their nations into wars. Be careful of what you believe, or it will take you down a path you don't want to go.

One may say that many evolutionists are highly intelligent and well-educated. Shouldn't they know what they're talking about? First, there are many creationists who are also highly intelligent and well-educated. Second, just because one is highly intelligent and well-educated doesn't necessarily make one correct. It's important to know why one believes as one does. Truth will always stand its ground. Closely examine the fossils, and one will find that they actually lend credence to creationism and not evolution.

Fossil research fails to produce transitional forms between major invertebrate types. The idea that the vertebrates evolved from the invertebrates also cannot be documented from fossil study. A.S. Romer's book, *Vertebrate Paleontology*, indicates that all major fish classes are clearly and distinctly set apart from one another with no transitional forms linking them.[60] Should not there be transitional evidence of these things if

---

[60] A.S. Romer, *Vertebrate Paleontology*, Third Edition (Chicago, Illinois: University of Chicago Press, 1966), p. 12.

evolution is true? In reality, quite the opposite is true. Fossil research indicates that life appears abruptly in diverse forms without evolutionary ancestors. This has been a great mystery to many evolutionists, but not to creationists.

Primate study is no different. Basically, lemurs, tarsiers, monkeys, apes, and man appear suddenly in the fossil record. Transitional forms between these basic types cannot be found. One may mention missing links like Australopithecus Man, Java Man, Peking Man, and Neanderthal Man; however, detailed study in each of these cases prove "prior human error" in assessments. I quote W.H. Rusch, one who has closely studied human fossils: "Therefore it may be concluded that fossil evidence offers no support for any schemes of the evolutionary descent of man, either hominid genera or from primate ancestors."[61]

Why do evolutionists fail to consider creation as an alternative to evolution? Perhaps it's based on humanistic, agnostic, or atheistic reasoning that doesn't want to acknowledge the existence of a Creator. I think some must reason that God doesn't exist, so they must somehow explain the development of man, and of course, evolution provides a so-called means to do this. Fortunately, for many in the scientific field given to this mindset, Charles Darwin came along and provided a source from which they could develop their explanations and justifications.

Although many would have you believe that all living things are interrelated and have evolved from a dead, inanimate world, don't buy into it. I close with a quote from Duane Gish, Ph.D., one who has thoroughly researched the subject. "After many years of intense study of the problem of origins from a scientific viewpoint, I am convinced that the facts of science declare special creation to be the only logical explanation of origins."[62] Fossil research soundly supports him.

---

[61] W.H. Rusch, "Human Fossils," in *Rock Strata and the Bible Record*, ed. P.A. Zimmerman (St. Louis, Missouri: Concordia Publishing House, 1970), p. 172.

[62] Duane T. Gish., Ph. D., *Evolution? The Fossils Say No!*, (San Diego, California: Institute for Creation Research Publishing, 1972), p. 174.

Simply put, there is no fossil evidence that man resulted from evolution. The missing links just don't exist period. Genesis 2:7 makes it clear, "And the Lord God formed man of the dust of the ground, and breathed into his nostrils the breath of life; and man became a living soul."

Final Score: Creationism (1); Evolution (0). Game over. Creationism wins now and in eternity.

The Grand Canyon

Chapter 23

Grand Canyon and Biblical Flood

One of the most outstanding sites that I've ever seen in my life was the Grand Canyon. I've traveled extensively throughout the world and have seen some pretty impressive sites; however, when I came up to the North Canyon Rim of the Grand Canyon and looked over the rail, I was awestruck.

The Grand Canyon is clearly an amazing creation. Of course, there are different views of how it was created over time. I, along with many others, believe that the biblical flood had a vast influence on its creation. For example, fossil-laden Redwall Limestone at Bright Angel Point in the Grand Canyon can be traced across the bulk of the continent and correlates with equivalent layers in Europe and the Himalayas in Asia.[63] I believe not only did the flood make mineral deposits from land areas miles away but it also carved the Grand Canyon terrain in a miraculous manner.

Consider also Zion National Park and the extensive Navajo Sandstone deposits. The grains of sand in its massive bed, which covers 140,000 square miles and is 2,200 feet thick, are believed to have come all the way from the Appalachian Mountains.[64] How else could such an enormous amount of sand have been transported across the continent except by a worldwide flood of epic proportions?

The biblical flood is key to unlocking the mysteries of these rock formations along with the mixed contents of layered deposits. The Bible not only provides direction for living but explains geological mysteries if we take time to look.

---

[63] "Along for the Ride" (Resource Preview), Answers IN GENESIS, Answers MAGAZINE, July 1, 2010, https://1ref.us/1bn (accessed Aug. 24, 2020).
[64] Ibid.

Tyrannosaurus Rex Skeleton

Chapter 24

Science Supports Noah's Flood

If dinosaurs died millions of years ago, according to evolutionists, then how can their fossils still contain soft tissue?

Within recent years, remarkable discoveries have been made in the study of dinosaur bones. Soft, unfossilized blood vessels and red blood cells have been discovered in dinosaur fossils. In 2005, a team of scientists led by paleontologist Mary Schweitzer found a femur of a Tyrannosaurus Rex that contained intact blood vessels and red blood cells. Once freed from the bones, the blood vessels could be stretched, and even snapped back into place. Further, Schweitzer and her colleagues also identified proteins from the Tyrannosaurus Rex femur.[65]

In 2008, paleontologist Thomas Kaye and his colleagues challenged Schweitzer's original findings. However, in early 2009, Schweitzer and her colleagues found a fossil of a duck-billed dinosaur that contained a host of soft-tissue structures. The analysis of this fossil, conducted by multiple independent laboratories, concluded that the fossil contained collagen, elastin, hemoglobin, and osteocytes.[66]

To get to the point, the claim of dinosaur soft tissue is real. Further, this discovery really seems logical if these bones were buried only a few thousand years ago during Noah's flood.

> Soft, unfossilized blood vessels and red blood cells have been discovered in dinosaur fossils.

Secular researchers have also dated Lyuba, a baby woolly mammoth, at 40,000 years old. Creationist researchers argue that this mammoth actually died around 2,000 B.C., during the Ice Age that followed Noah's flood.[67] Lyuba's remarkable lack of decay strongly supports a death much more in line with the biblical timescale.

Scientific evidence supports the biblical story of Noah's flood.

---

[65] "TWO: Those Not-So-Dry Bones," Answers IN GENESIS, Answers MAGAZINE, by Dr. Marcus Ross, January 1, 2010, https://1ref.us/1bo (accessed Aug. 24, 2020).
[66] Ibid.
[67] "Mammoth Tour," Answers IN GENESIS, Answers MAGAZINE, April 1, 2010, https://1ref.us/1bp (accessed Aug. 24, 2020).

Alaskan Glaciers

Chapter 25

Noah's Flood and the Great Ice Age

••

Much debate has taken place over the Great Ice Age. Different theories have been proposed and discussed throughout time on this subject. However, I believe that there are definitive answers for strong consideration.

With that in mind, there's something that stays with me as I approach life. When something happens to one significantly in life, one should always refer to the Bible for guidance. I know that it has been my foundation for living. What does the Bible say about different situations? Equally, what does the Bible say about certain phenomena throughout time?

Based on the Bible, over 4,000 years ago, God judged the wickedness on the earth. Many believe that Noah's flood occurred somewhere between 3,000 and 2,000 B.C. One must consider that this Great Deluge destroyed everything on land because of the persuasiveness, and depth, of the water coverage over the earth. This makes sense.

> **Genesis 7:11** says, "In the six hundredth year of Noah's life, in the second month, the seventeenth day of the month, the same day were **all the fountains of the great deep broken up, and the windows of heaven were opened**."

This indicates that fountains from below the surface broke up, and the windows of heaven were opened. This means enormous volumes of water came forth from beneath the surface of the earth and from the above atmosphere. The rainfall must have been immense, to say the least.

Huge earthquakes could have caused great rifts in the earth's crust, exploding the release of waters from beneath and setting off volcanic activity. When the earth opened up, coupled with seismic plate shifts, volcanos probably erupted and put hot lava and volcanic ash and dust into the atmosphere.

Interbedded within the sedimentary rocks is evidence of incredible volcanic activity that has no parallel today. Vast, unusually thick layers of volcanic flows and ash interlayer sedimentary rocks fit the worldwide flood paradigm very well. It appears that at the end of the flood, the world was covered by huge volumes of volcanic ash and gas that had spewed into the atmosphere.[68] This volcanic ash and dust would naturally block the warmth of the sun from reaching the surface of the denuded earth.

---

[68] "Chapter 7—The Genesis Flood Caused the Ice Age," Answers IN GENESIS, "Frozen In Time," by Michael J. Oard, October 1, 2004, https://1ref.us/1bq (accessed

Now consider the remaining water bodies (oceans, seas, lakes, rivers, ponds) that had been warmed from all the volcanic activity. These water bodies then send warm water vapor into the atmosphere. With cold air already over the land, mixing with warm water vapor, then one has the potential for great snowfall.

With the atmosphere filled with volcanic ash and dust shielding warmth from the sun reaching the earth, then the snow remains and builds, and eventually, sheets of ice develop in great portions of the earth.

One may recall when Mount St. Helens erupted on May 18, 1980, that volcanic ash and dust were blown thousands of feet into the air and eventually spread extensively to multiple states. Sunlight was greatly shielded as one revisits this scene. This was just from one mountain erupting. Imagine multiple, and even stronger and more intense eruptions, happening throughout the earth during the Great Flood. Then consider the extensive amount of time it would take for the fallout to settle.

David Keys makes a case that a massive volcanic eruption in Indonesia caused the darkness, cooling, crop failures, and social upheaval that was recorded in 535 A.D.[69]

My point is that there is a viable biblical explanation for the Great Ice Age. Much more can be discussed on the Great Ice Age; however, if you research this subject in greater detail, you'll find additional detailed information supportive of this narrative—that the Great Ice Age followed Noah's flood.

September 18, 2020).
[69] Ibid.

Niagara Falls

Chapter 26

God Has Revealed Himself to Creation

••

Although many people have not read the Bible, I know that all people have read his other book, the *Splendor of Creation*, which conveys exceedingly imaginative and breathtaking scenes beyond description within its most thoroughly creative pages. I, for one, have been so impressed by its contents on numerous occasions. I've seen the sun rise and set over the horizon while onboard a ship in the ocean. I've stood at the rim of the

Grand Canyon with awestruck impressions. I've watched tons of water pour over Niagara Falls into the gorge below with its rising mist.

Who can explain the hues of Arizona's Painted Desert, or the grandeur of an Alaskan night with its myriad of stars on display? Who can explain the majesty and strength built into the Rocky Mountains or the pounding surf splashing onto the picturesque and rocky coastline of Northern California? It's quite clear that God has unmistakably revealed Himself to all in creation.

I then realize that man's blood system is more complex than anything man has ever created with his limited, intelligent mind. I then consider all the biological, ecological, and geological systems throughout the world and how they interrelate with such precision. I consider it amazing how gravity and centrifugal force maintain such dynamic balance on each other. Most assuredly, the *Splendor of Creation* is exhaustive in the revelation of its author.

I consider all the mammal, fowl, and fish species throughout the world. Each species has varied and detailed patterns of living with amazing colorful and functional designs. The creativity and imagination of all this is UNEQUIVOCALLY UNMATCHED.

I look up on a clear night and see a multitude of stars hung on nothing. How can this be? Who painted these beautiful constellations with no canvas? Finite minds cannot explain this because it's supernatural beyond human comprehension.

There's another interesting facet to the *Splendor of Creation*. It's a fantastic book that continuously reveals new chapters in awesome discoveries of splendor. In other words, it's full of life with new discoveries waiting to be found on a daily and regular basis. What an amazing book!

How then can an atheist who has read the same book then say that there is no God?

Chapter 27

Humans Created in the Image of God

....

Genesis 1:26–27—"And God said, **Let us make man in our image**, after our likeness: and let them have dominion over the fish of the sea, and over the fowl of the air, and over the cattle, and over all the earth, and over every creeping thing that creepeth upon the earth. **So God created man in his own image**, in the image of God created he him; male and female created he them."

No creature is designed like a human being. Our ability to communicate, understand, feel emotions, and to think logically seems to demonstrate that we were created for a particular purpose. Evolutionists, however, believe that human beings just evolved with no special design or purpose. Which is true?

Humans are creative, emotional, and spiritual beings, very distinctive from the animal kingdom. Humans have the unique ability to communicate thoughts and emotions through meaningful verbiage. Consider how human speech and writing contain complex sounds, developed thoughts, and an abundance of words. Notice that humans have a noticeably long throat, flexible tongue, defined, shaped lips, and distinct vocal cords. There's flexibility in the mouth, tongue, and lips to create a wide spectrum of sounds. A multitude of muscles work together during communication, while the brain and neurons process information and actions at a tremendous rate of speed. Verbal skills like these don't just evolve from monkeys.

Consider how humans are capable of a wide range of emotions, ranging from jubilation to desperation. Then consider how the different ways of expressing emotions set humans apart from animals. The limbic system is a group of interconnected structures located deep within the brain; it's the part of the brain that's responsible for behavioral and emotional responses for humans.

Humans derive pleasure in many unique ways. Things are appreciated through the five human senses—sight, hearing, touch, smell, and taste. Humans may stop to marvel at a great man-made structure like the pyramids in Giza, or a beautiful scene from nature like the Niagara Falls, while animals won't process in like manner.

Humans also exhibit perceptive thought and conscious behavior. Animals are different in that they're more programmed to instinctive behavior. The migration of birds proves this point as they fly thousands of miles in their annual travels, often traveling the same route year after year with hardly any deviation. Their instinctive clock kicks in, and they're off.

Further, consider the number of extensive and verified cases of one's spirit leaving one's body in hospital emergency room situations.

Numerous people can tell you what they saw when their spirits left their bodies during those periods of time. Yes, man has a spirit, also known as one's conscience.

Why was man created? He was created to know and glorify God in a personal relationship. Numerous scriptures from the Bible support this revelation.

Chapter 28

Breath of Life

∙∙∙

There's something exceptionally intriguing about life and the willingness to live. Whether it be in human beings or the animal kingdom, species strive to survive. Creatures regularly seek food and water in their efforts to subsist. Notice how endangering situations are carefully avoided when life is threatened. Dangerous situations are clearly shunned in efforts for protection of life.

God is so awesome. He created life, and I'm quite sure that He put this instinct in species; however, there's another aspect to life and God in regard to the breath of life. Let's take the subject of a human being born. I personally believe that God breathes life into that body at conception. At death, I believe that breath of life is drawn back into God, leaving just a corpse and departure of the person's spirit. In essence, God is the breath of life. Without His breath of life into a body, there could be no life for He is the complete source of life. Please consider the following scriptures:

> **Genesis 2:7**—"And the Lord God formed man of the dust of the ground, and **breathed into his nostrils the breath of life**; and man became a living soul."
>
> **Job 33:4**—"The spirit of God hath made me, and **the breath of the Almighty hath given me life**."
>
> **Psalm 104:29**—"Thou hidest thy face, they are troubled: **thou takest away their breath, they die**, and return to their dust."

This, in essence, separates species from inanimate objects, so to speak. Without the breath of life into a species, that species would be just a collection of matter with no feelings of existence whatsoever. It would be inanimate, and basically, just occupy a space like a rock. The breath of life from God cannot be covered by science textbooks. It cannot be covered by evolution. It defies humanistic definition because it extends from deity in the fullest sense of the word.

Chapter 29

The Bible

• •

The Bible contains the Old and New Testaments. It consists of sixty-six books, thirty-nine books in the Old Testament, and twenty-seven books in the New Testament. It was written over a span of 1500 years (from circa 1400 B.C to A.D. 100). It had about forty authors and written by people with diverse occupational backgrounds. It was written on three different continents over the course of many centuries. Most was written in what is modern-day Israel (Asia); however, some passages of Jeremiah were written in Egypt (Africa) and several New Testament epistles were written in Europe. It was also written in different languages.

There is a natural unity of the books and how they interrelate. There is wisdom throughout its pages as one examines the details of the writings.

Given the aforementioned, and coupled with prophetic fulfillment as proven throughout history, and archeological evidence support, I submit to you that it is the inspired Word of God. As such, it should be highly valued, believed, and accepted into one's heart for admonition, acceptance, guidance, reverence, and repentance.

> One needs to view the Bible as truth, and truth is absolute.

One needs to view the Bible as truth, and truth is absolute. It always proves its course. The Bible should become one's foundation for living, and compass to navigate all of life's days.

Yes, there is a God. Make no mistake—He's real indeed. Let me say it this way—

God's Word: Bulletproof!

*Section Four—*Miscellaneous Commentaries

Resurrection

Chapter 30

Prophecy and Calculations

∙∙

Dr. Peter W. Stoner published a book called *Science Speaks* in 1952 with further printings in time. Based on his background, he was an extremely experienced mathematician. He was the Chairman of the Departments of Mathematics and Astronomy at Pasadena City College until 1953, and then became Chairman of the Science Division at Westmont College.

Although there are many Messianic prophecies, Dr. Stoner is perhaps best known for his analysis of just eight of them from his book *Science*

Speaks. As he applied the modern science of probability to these eight prophecies regarding Christ, he says, "**The chance that any man might have ... fulfilled all eight prophecies is one in 10^{17}. That would be one in 100,000,000,000,000,000.**" (One hundred quadrillion).[70]

The following is a great illustration of the magnitude of this number. Stoner suggests that "we take 10^{17}. silver dollars and lay them on the face of Texas. They will cover all of the state two feet deep. Now, mark one of these silver dollars and stir the whole mass thoroughly ... Blindfold a man and tell him he can travel as far as he wishes, but he must pick up [that one marked silver dollar.]"[71] What chance would he have of getting the right one?" Astronomically and unequivocally unlikely.

Stoner then concludes, "Just the same chance that the prophets would have had of writing those eight prophecies and having them all come true in any one man, ... providing they wrote using their own wisdom."[72]

Let me say it this way—**The fulfillment of Bible prophecy in the life of Jesus proves that the death, burial, and resurrection occurred, and that Jesus is God in the flesh. Accept it, receive it, and believe it.**

Dr. Stoner also analyzed major Bible prophecies and associated probability calculations concerning cities and nations. These included Tyre, Samaria, Gaza and Ashkelon, Jericho, Moab and Ammon, Edom, and Babylon. Again, the probability calculations for prophecy fulfillment are staggering above staggering.

Dr. Stoner even analyzed how the Bible was devoid of scientific error. He pointed out that his copy of Young's *General Astronomy*, released in 1898, was full of errors. I say that because the Bible was written many hundreds of years ago.

---

[70] Stoner, Peter W. and Newman, Robert C., *Science Speaks (Online Edition): Scientific Proof of the Accuracy of Prophecy and the Bible*, Chicago, IL., Moody Press, 2002, Online Edition, Chapter Three, Revision Nov. 2005, revised and HTML formatted, by Donald W. Stoner. https://1ref.us/1br (accessed Aug. 28, 2020).
[71] Ibid.
[72] Ibid.

Consider just some of the many things that the Bible foretold before man ever knew about them. These items are referred to or supported by scripture.[73]

- The Contour of the earth is circular (see Isa. 40:22)
- Life is in the blood (see Lev. 17:11, 14)
- Bodies are comprised from earthen elements (see Gen. 2:7; 3:19)
- Gravity is relevant (see Job 26:7)
- Wind has direction (see Eccles. 1:6)
- Ocean currents are anticipated (Ps. 8:8)
- A rain cycle exists (see Isa. 55:10)
- There is physical law and energy dynamics (see Ps. 102:25–26)
- Mountains on ocean floor exist (see Jonah 2:5–6)
- Light can be divided (see Job 38:24)
- Reproduction is explained (see Gen. 1:27–28, 2:24)
- Ice age is inferred (see Job 38:29–30)
- Life begins at fertilization (see Jer. 1:5)
- Air has weight (see Job 28:25)
- Bible describes dinosaurs (see Job 40:15–24)
- Seeds of plants contain its life (see Gen. 1:11, 29)
- Safe drinking water is explained (see Lev. 11:33–36)
- Visible matter is comprised of invisible elements (see Heb. 11:3)
- Germs exist (see Lev. 15:13)
- Ideal dimensions for a water vessel are given (see Gen. 6:15)
- Oceans contain springs (see Job 38:16)
- Origin of rainbows explained (see Gen. 9:13–16)
- God fashions and knits us together in the womb (see Job 10:8–12, 31:15)
- Continental drift is inferred (Gen. 7:11)

---

[73] "101 Scientific Facts & Foreknowledge", Eternal Productions, https://1ref.us/1bt (accessed Sept. 20, 2020).

Dr. Stoner further discusses how God used the amazing and remarkable intricacies of radiation energy, kinetic energy, and gravitation in the act of creation.

Let me say it this way—**The Bible is divinely inspired from the hand of God. Accept it, receive it, and believe it.**

Jezreel Valley

Chapter 31

Discovery of Oil in Israel?

Some oil has already been discovered in Israel; however, I believe there will be a coming and more massive discovery of oil in the future. The Valley of Jezreel is located near Megiddo in Israel. It's a lush, green valley that has endured wars in the past and will host the greatest of wars in the future. You see, according to the Bible, this is the area where Armageddon will take place. As I think of this location, I ponder what will bring the forces of the world into this area.

Of course, many nations that surround Israel would like to see her cast into the sea, due to ethnic and religious reasons; however, there is another catalyst that many have failed to recognize. That catalyst is oil. Someday, and I believe sooner than many think, oil is going to be abundantly discovered in Israel.

Consider the story of Sodom and Gomorrah. Could a tremendous explosion blowing tons of rock and dirt skyward, leaving a gaping hole with great width and depth, have caused the formation of the Dead Sea? Could it have been the ignition of a huge quantity of underground methane gas and oil? After all, this is in the area, where formerly Sodom, Gomorrah, and the Valley of Siddim were located. Throughout this region there were numerous oil pockets and wells that were on ground level, which is proven both historically and biblically.

> **Genesis 19:24–25** says, "Then the LORD **rained upon Sodom and upon Gomorrah brimstone and fire from the LORD out of heaven**; And he overthrew those cities, and all the plain, and all the inhabitants of the cities, and that which grew upon the ground."

> **Genesis 14:10** further says, "And the **vale of Siddim was full of slimepits**; and the kings of Sodom and Gomorrah fled, and fell there; and they that remained fled to the mountain." "Slimepits" are also translated "bitumen" or "tar pits" in other translations.

> Now, consider **Ezekiel 16:53**, "When I shall bring again their captivity, **the captivity of Sodom and her daughters**, and the captivity of Samaria and her daughters, then will I bring again the captivity of thy captives in the midst of them:"—"the captivity" is also translated "fortunes" in other translations.

In 1948, Israel became a nation again. I believe the discovery of oil is not far off. Most assuredly, the fortunes of Sodom were not rocks, grains of sand, nor pebbles. I personally believe oil is involved here.

Much rock that is mined from the Dead Sea is saturated with oil, and could feasibly be mined as shale oil. Deep ravines surround this area where oil seeps are quite noticeable. The indicators are there for a potential massive discovery.

One of the greatest preservatives and natural containers known to man is salt. During past years, it has proven to be a trap for oil deposits in many places in the world. A huge salt deposit currently exists in the area of Sodom and Gomorrah and could have trapped enormous amounts of oil for the latter-day use of Israel. I believe time will prove this to be correct. Could I be wrong in my interpretation or perception? Possibly so, but I don't think I am.

Consider that, just before the Jews returned in 1948, Israel was primarily swamp or barren desert. The Jews, through ingenuity and arduous work, have amazingly turned this tiny nation into an exceptionally productive and agriculturally efficient country. Israel is now a big exporter of fruits and vegetables to Russia and Europe. **Isaiah 27:6** foretold, "He shall cause them that come of Jacob to take root: **Israel shall blossom and bud, and fill the face of the world with fruit.**"

> **Isaiah 45:3** further says, "And **I will give thee the treasures of darkness, and hidden riches of secret places**, that thou mayest know that I, the LORD, which call thee by thy name, am the God of Israel." Although this scripture was spoken to Cyrus, I do believe that the treasures of darkness are not that far off for Israel in the form of oil.

Discovery of a vast supply of oil in Israel would have worldwide strategic, geopolitical, and economic implications. Be assured, major secular news and media organizations will quickly and pervasively broadcast this discovery. Although much of the secular world will not see God's hand in this whole affair, many will truly acknowledge the glory and honor of God, who keeps His covenant.

The world's demand for oil is ever-growing. It's a precious commodity that nations fight wars over. Could a massive discovery of oil in Israel be further reason for nations to converge on this tiny country?

I personally believe that oil will be discovered in Israel in much greater deposits in the future in accordance with God's timetable and fulfillment of His Word (fortunes of Sodom). That said, look for it sometime in the future, and ultimately, to become another catalyst towards the road to Armageddon.

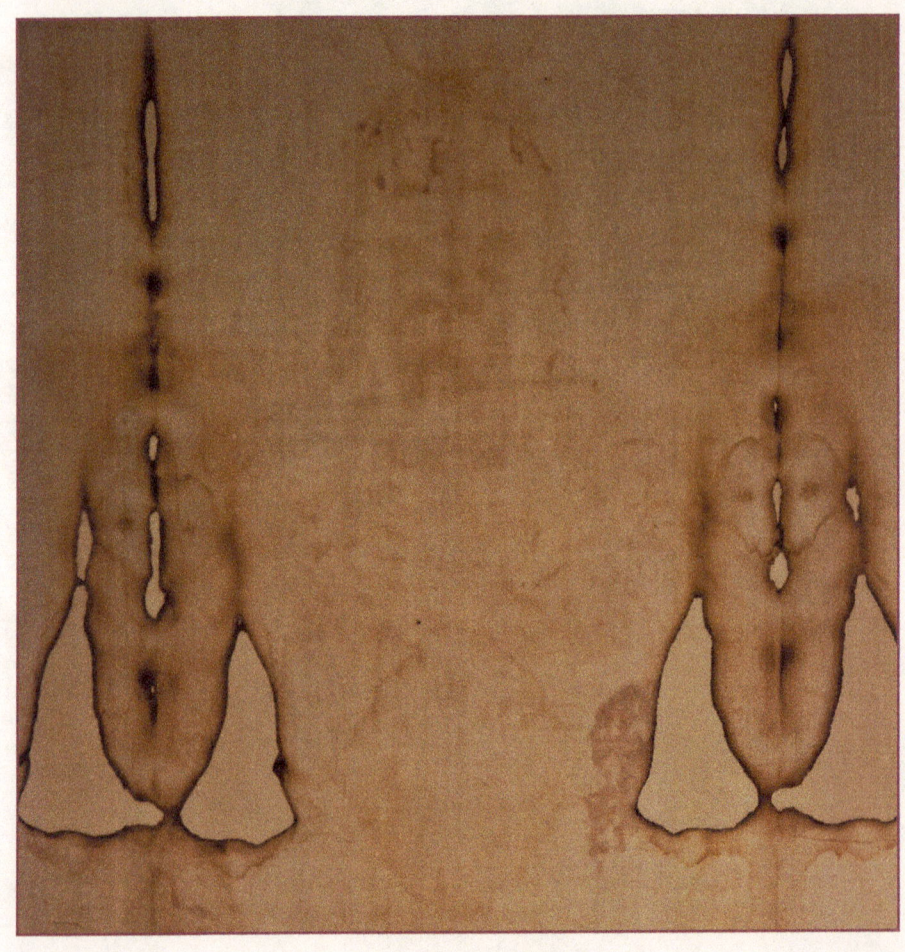

Shroud of Turin

Chapter 32

The Shroud of Turin

···

T he Shroud of Turin is a length of linen bearing the negative of a man. Some claim the image depicts Jesus Christ, and that the fabric is the burial shroud in which He was wrapped after His crucifixion. Diverse arguments have been made in scientific and popular publications claiming to prove or disprove that the cloth is the authentic burial shroud of Jesus based on disciplines ranging from chemistry to biology and medical forensics to optical image analysis.

Technical progress made it possible for a photograph of the Turin Shroud. The photographic plate converted the impressions on the cloth into black and white. A face became clearly visible. Specialists all over the world studied the amazing photograph. Attempts made by painters showed that no artist was able to convert a human face by the processes of the mind into a negative image and paint it. This shroud could not have been a forgery.[74]

In 1988, Carbon-14 dating tests were done and dated a corner piece of the shroud to be from the Middle Ages between the years 1260 and 1390. Since that time, newer experiments/testing have taken place, and these tests refute the 1988 tests and place the Shroud of Turin into the First century A.D. time period.

Some key observations are as follows:[75]

- As an ancient textile, the stitching pattern is quite similar to the hem of a cloth found in the tombs of the Jewish fortress of Masada. The Masada cloth dates to between 40 B.C. and A.D. 73. This kind of stitch has never been found in Medieval Europe.
- No one knows for sure how the images were created. The images are scorch-like, yet not created by heat, and are a purely surface phenomenon limited to the crowns of the top fibers.
- The Shroud is clearly not a painting; no evidence of pigments or media was found.

---

[74] Werner Keller, *The Bible As History* (New York, NY: William Morrow and Company, Inc., 1981), p. 355.

[75] "The Shroud of Turin—Evidence it is authentic," Original text by John C. Iannone 1999–2001. Adapted by J.M. Fischer from 2004 to 2016, https://1ref.us/1bs (accessed Aug. 28, 2020).

- Most bloodstains on the Shroud are exudates from clotted wounds transferred to the cloth by contact with a wounded human body. The blood was on the cloth before the image.
- The blood on the Shroud is real; human male blood of type AB.
- The image on the Shroud is of a man 5 feet 10 1/2 inches tall, about 175 pounds, covered with scourge wounds and bloodstains.
- Numerous surgeons and pathologists agree that the words of the New Testament regarding the Passion clearly match the wounds depicted on the Shroud and that these wounds are consistent with the weapons used by ancient Roman soldiers in crucifixion.
- The burial is consistent with ancient Jewish burial customs in all respects, including the use of cave-tombs, attitude of the body (hands folded over loins), and types of burial cloths.

Matthew 27:59–60, **Mark 15:46**, and **Luke 23:53** state that Joseph of Arimathea wrapped the body of Jesus in a piece of linen cloth and placed it in a new tomb. **John 19:38–40** refers to cloths of linen used by Joseph of Arimathea and states that Peter found multiple pieces of burial cloth after the tomb was observed opened, cloths of linen for the body and a separate cloth for the head in **John 20:6–7**.

> These wounds are consistent with the weapons used by ancient Roman soldiers in crucifixion.

Is this a burial cloth for Jesus? I cannot attest that it is or isn't. Some analysts believe that it is, some analysts believe that it's not. I included a chapter on the Turin Shroud because numerous analysts greatly researched the image, and as such, this drew immense attention to Jesus.

My point is that people were focused on Jesus. Jesus was not a myth by any means. He was a reality. He lived, died, was buried in a tomb, and He rose again in accordance with the scriptures. They're using all this information in their analysis.

As these analysts focused on the Shroud of Turin and its possible relationship to Jesus, we need to focus on our relationship to Jesus in earnestness. We need to focus on the reality that He died, was buried, and resurrected in accordance with the scriptures for our salvation. Prophetic fulfillment, archeological evidence, science, and common sense reasoning unequivocally prove the Word of God. The question is—what are we going to do about Jesus in your lives? It's time for us to accept the truth of God's Word. It's time for us to focus on the reality of our relationship with Jesus once and for all and receive Him as our Lord and Savior. **It's TIME**. Now, please proceed to the conclusion, the most important part of this book.

Conclusion

This book discussed prophetic fulfillment, archeological evidence, and science and common sense reasoning in support of the Bible. Volumes could be written on each of these areas; however, I believe enough was discussed to prove the validity of the Bible, and the importance of the salvation message. Therefore, I now want to get to the most important part of this book. **If there is any doubt as to your eternal destiny or salvation, then today, I urge you to consider the following scriptures. Accept them, receive them, and believe them.**

> "As it is written, There is none righteous, no, not one" **(Rom. 3:10).**

> "For all have sinned, and come short of the glory of God" **(Rom. 3:23).**

> "For the wages of sin is death; but the gift of God is eternal life through Jesus Christ our Lord" **(Rom. 6:23).**

> "For there is one God, and one mediator between God and men, the man Christ Jesus" **(1 Tim. 2:5).**

> "That if thou shalt confess with thy mouth the Lord Jesus, and shalt believe in thine heart that God hath raised him from the dead, thou shalt be saved. For with the heart man believeth unto

righteousness; and with the mouth confession is made unto salvation" **(Rom. 10:9–10).**

Now, here's a Sinner's Prayer to receive Jesus as Lord and Savior. Please repeat the following prayer and mean it from your heart. You must be sincere, or they will only be words and mean nothing. If you are sincere, then God is sincere because God always honors His Word.

"Dear Heavenly Father, I come to You in the name of the Lord Jesus Christ. I ask You to forgive me of all my sins. I accept Jesus as my Lord and Savior and believe in my heart that He died on the cross for my sins and that You raised Him from the dead so that I could have right standing with You. I now repent and confess Jesus as my Lord and Savior. I thank You for giving me eternal salvation and ask that You would help me in my Christian walk."

I strongly encourage you to read your Bible daily to get to know the Lord better, talk to God daily in prayer, and find a church where the Bible is taught as the complete Word of God. I also encourage you to be water baptized.

About the Author

Commander Michael H. Imhof, U.S. Navy (ret.), and former Navy SEAL, was born in Fort Bragg, North Carolina, and raised in Blasdell, New York. He attended the State University College of New York at Buffalo, where he received a bachelor of science degree. He was commissioned in 1973. After completing Basic Underwater Demolition/SEAL training in Coronado, California, Commander Imhof was assigned to SEAL Team TWO, subsequent Naval Special Warfare commands, and other duty assignments.

Commander Imhof, possessing a Naval Special Warfare designator, has served throughout the world in numerous positions. Assignments include Platoon Commander, Training Officer, Operations Officer, Staff Officer, Executive Officer, and Commanding Officer. A graduate of the U.S. Army Special Forces Officer Qualification Course, he also earned a master's degree in administration from George Washington University and served as an instructor at the U.S. Naval Academy. He has numerous service awards.

He has lived in Egypt, Jordan, Israel, Panama, South Korea, Liberia, Sudan, Somalia, Sinai, and Afghanistan besides serving in numerous other countries throughout the world. On December 17, 1981, he was hijacked in Southern Lebanon while on duty with the United Nations Truce Supervision Organization. He believes his later escape was truly a blessing of God. A military officer of strong Christian convictions, Commander Imhof is ready and willing to share his faith with all. He is convinced that the Bible is the authoritative and uncompromised Word of God and gives thanks for the wonderful blessings of God in his life. He is the author of six Christian books.

Additional Books by Author

STAND UP FOR GOD

This 66-page book discusses biblical principles learned in a military career. Travel with Commander Michael Imhof around the globe and learn about what it means to *Stand Up for God*. The former U.S. Navy SEAL shares his many experiences including Basic Underwater Demolition/SEAL training, being **HIJACKED** in Southern Lebanon, assignments at SEAL commands, and working with officers from the Soviet Union. These vivid stories, plus many more, will show the reader what it's like to be a fearless Christian in a sinful and selfish world. Material is written in simplicity and with clarity. It's outstanding reading and has something of interest for all. ISBN 978-1-4796-0847-8; Aspect Books (www.aspectbooks.com)

SUPERNATURAL TESTIMONIES

This 152-page book has twenty-nine testimonies of people from a broad spectrum of different lifestyles.

Read about how the manifested love of God set people free from bondage, deception, and desperate situations.

The writer says, "The people in these testimonies came to realize that there was a void in their lives. So many times people look back over their lives and realize that God was tugging on their hearts all the time, but they wouldn't listen. Thus, people go their ways, make poor decisions, and plunge into sin. As a result, people often call out to God in desperate situations."

ISBN 1-933858-02-8; Evangel Press

TESTIMONIES OF EX-MUSLIMS

This 69-page book has eighteen testimonies of Muslims who left the Islamic faith and made their decision for Christianity. The content and style of these chapters has been presented the way the people have presented their testimonies. Read of how God moves on hearts who truly desire to know Him, regardless of the severe persecution and consequences.

The writer says, "I was living in Afghanistan when the idea came to me about putting together a small book of testimonies from ex-Muslims. Many people have been so misled by the religion of Islam. In many cases, Muslims are very sincere in their beliefs, but that does not make their beliefs correct. Truth, in reality, is more important than sincerity."

ISBN 1-933858-01-X; Evangel Press

WALKING WITH GOD

This 188-page daily devotional in poetic form conveys truths of the Bible and how they apply to life in the area of successful everyday living.

The author says, "In reality, each daily reading provides distinct and positive direction, much like a small sermon. Value the truths of the Bible, for the Bible is a special gift to man. It always leads us to victory because God is a good God and only wants the best for us."

ISBN 1-57258-222-7; Aspect Books (www.aspectbooks.com)

LESSONS FROM BIBLE CHARACTERS

This 57-page book is a straightforward analysis of Biblical characters and situations that inspire both teens and adults.

The purpose of this book is to examine thirty-five situations where we can learn from Bible characters. In Chapter 28 titled "Faith Pays Off," the author writes about a specific Bible character then states, "Let us also not allow temporal circumstances, no matter what they are, prevent us from receiving from God. The storms of life or adversities say one thing but the Word of God says victory."

ISBN 1-57258-019-4; Teach Services, Inc. (www.teachservices.com); also available in Spanish.

MORE LESSONS FROM BIBLE CHARACTERS

This 64-page book gives insightful analysis of Biblical characters and situations that bring encouragement both teens and adults.

The author writes, "Thirty-five situations are examined, and again, short summaries and simple conclusions are made for everyday living."

In Chapter 19 titled "Love Is an Action Word," the author analyzes a Bible character, then writes, "Love truly makes a difference in lives, for those in need of it and for those giving it. We're the better for it as we put love into action."

ISBN 1-57258-205-7; Teach Services, Inc. (www.teachservices.com); also available in Spanish.

Contact Information

EVANGELIST: Michael H. Imhof is an **EVANGELIST**. His goal is to speak before congregations, where God opens the doors for him. That said, his background is unique versus most. He's a **retired U.S. Navy Commander and a former Navy SEAL**. He has lived and worked in a multitude of countries in the world on different continents, including Muslim countries.

He has spoken in numerous churches and different denominations throughout the United States and outside America on varied subjects over time. He speaks at men's events and also conducts revival meetings. He has a fervent heart for the things of God. He firmly believes that Jesus Christ is the way of salvation. If one does not find Jesus Christ in this lifetime as Lord and Savior, one will not find him in the next.

A dynamic speaker, Commander Imhof, under the inspiration of the Holy Spirit, uses his unique background and many experiences in encouraging, edifying, and inspiring others in the things of God. Anytime he's behind the pulpit, he seeks for the Holy Spirit to speak through him. When he finishes ministering, he wants lives changed for God's glory. He gives God all the praise.

BASIC MISSION: Salvation of souls for God's kingdom and to assist/educate/encourage people in the things of God.

WEBSITE: www.michaelimhofministries.org

SPEAKING ENGAGEMENTS: Feel free to contact Commander (Evangelist) Michael H. Imhof via website for speaking engagements.

ASPECT Books
www.ASPECTBooks.com

We invite you to view the complete
selection of titles we publish at:
www.ASPECTBooks.com

We encourage you to write us
with your thoughts about this,
or any other book we publish at:
info@ASPECTBooks.com

ASPECT Books' titles may be purchased in
bulk quantities for educational, fund-raising,
business, or promotional use.
bulksales@ASPECTBooks.com

Finally, if you are interested in seeing
your own book in print, please contact us at:
publishing@ASPECTBooks.com

We are happy to review your manuscript at no charge.

www.ingramcontent.com/pod-product-compliance
Lightning Source LLC
Chambersburg PA
CBHW071444160426
43195CB00013B/2023